The Usborne
Little Book
of
London

Rosie Dickins
Designed by Brian Voakes and Linda Penny

Photography by Stef Lumley
Illustrated by Ian Jackson

London Consultant: Peter Matthews, Museum of London

Contents

Internet links

Throughout this book we have recommended websites where you can find out more about famous places and things to do in London. To visit the sites, go to the **Usborne Quicklinks Website** where you will find links to all the sites.

1. Go to www.usborne-quicklinks.com
2. Type the keyword for this book: **london**
3. Type the page number of the link you want to visit.
4. Click on the links to go to the recommended sites.

Here are some of the things you can do on the websites recommended in this book:

- See photographs and panoramic views of London taken from the London Eye.
- Hear bells and singing from Westminster Abbey and take an interactive tour.
- Browse online collections at the Science Museum and the National Gallery.
- Take a virtual tour of the Globe Theatre.
- Play games to find your way on the London Underground.
- Discover online dinosaur activities at the Natural History Museum.

Site availability

The links in Usborne Quicklinks are regularly reviewed and updated, but occasionally you may get a message that a site is unavailable. This might be temporary, so try again later, or even the next day. Websites do occasionally close down and when this happens, we will replace them with new links in Usborne Quicklinks. Sometimes we add extra links too, if we think they are useful. So when you visit Usborne Quicklinks, the links may be slightly different from those described in your book.

Downloadable pictures

Pictures marked with a ✿ in this book can be downloaded from the Usborne Quicklinks Website. These pictures are for personal use only and must not be used for commercial purposes.

Safety on the Internet

Ask your parent's or guardian's permission before you connect to the Internet and make sure you follow these simple rules:

- Never give out information about yourself, such as your real name, address, phone number or the name of your school.
- If a site asks you to log in or register by typing your name or email address, ask permission from an adult first.

What you need

To visit the websites you need a computer with an Internet connection and a web browser (the software that lets you look at information on the Internet). Some sites need extra programs (plug-ins) to play sound or show videos or animations.

If you go to a site and do not have the necessary plug-in, a message will come up on the screen. There is usually a link to click on to download the plug-in. For more information about plug-ins, go to Usborne Quicklinks and click on "Net Help".

Notes for parents and guardians

The websites described in this book are regularly reviewed, but the content of a website may change at any time and Usborne Publishing is not responsible for the content on any website other than its own.

We recommend that children are supervised while on the Internet, that they do not use Internet chat rooms, and that you use Internet filtering software to block unsuitable material. Please ensure that your children read and follow the safety guidelines printed above. For more information, see the Net Help area on the Usborne Quicklinks Website.

COMPUTER NOT ESSENTIAL
If you don't have access to the Internet, don't worry. On its own, this book is an excellent guide to London.

About London

London began in Roman times as a small town, but it has grown over the centuries into a huge city with a population of over seven million people. Over the next few pages, you can read more about historic London and how it became the city you see today. Later in the book, you can find out about London's many open spaces, museums, shops, markets and its people, traditions and festivals.

This map shows how London has grown over the centuries from a small Roman town, to the huge, sprawling city it is today.

| Roman city | 1500s | 1700s |
| 1800s | London today | |

The capital city

London is the capital city of Great Britain, which means it is the home of parliament and the ruling king or queen. London has not always been a capital city, however. In Roman times, the capital was a town called Colchester. Later, London grew in size and importance, overtaking Colchester.

Why London grew

London grew because of the River Thames. The river allowed ships to reach the city, making it a busy port. The roads and railways helped London grow, too. London has grown very fast since the nineteenth century. Nearby towns were swallowed up by the city, forming the area known as Greater London. Today, more than seven million people live in Greater London.

The White Tower at the Tower of London

Roman London

People have lived in the London area for more than 5,000 years, but there used to be forests and marshes instead of a city. London itself was begun by the Romans about 2,000 years ago. They called their town Londinium.

Queen Boudicca fought the Romans. You can see this statue of her by Westminster Bridge.

Soldiers and settlers

Roman soldier

Roman ships

Londinium in flames

The Roman wall today

In the first century, Roman soldiers came to take over Britain. Some of them settled by the Thames and built Londinium. This was the beginning of London.

Roman ships sailed up the Thames, bringing supplies. The Romans built a bridge over the Thames, and there has been a bridge in the same area ever since.

A native people called the Iceni attacked the Romans. The Iceni, led by Queen Boudicca, set fire to Londinium and killed everyone in the town.

In the end, the Romans defeated Boudicca and Londinium was built again. A wall was built around the new town. You can still see parts of the wall today.

Inside Londinium

Inside the wall, Londinium had houses, bath houses, temples, shops and markets. Nowadays, this area is a business district, known as the City.

The picture on the right shows how part of Londinium, the Basilica (business area) and Forum (market place), might have looked.
The Basilica and Forum were at the heart of Roman life. They stood where Gracechurch Street, in the City, is today. You can find out more about Roman life at the Museum of London (see page 61).

Basilica

Columns

Shops and workshops

Forum

Vases made by Roman craftsmen

Anglo-Saxon London

You can see many Anglo-Saxon treasures in London museums; the helmet above is on display at the British Museum.

At the end of the fourth century, the Roman Empire began to fall apart and the Romans left Britain. People called Angles, Saxons and Jutes then came to Britain from Holland, Germany and Denmark. Together, these peoples are called the Anglo-Saxons.

Roman ruins

Londinium in ruins

After the Romans left, Londinium probably lay in ruins. The city grew up again, however, because it was a useful port.

Saint Paul's

Monks in Saint Paul's

Many people became Christians. In 604, the first Saint Paul's Cathedral was built. There is still a Saint Paul's on this site today.

Viking attacks

Viking ships

In the ninth and tenth centuries, London was attacked by Danish Vikings who sailed up the river to the city and settled there.

London Bridge is falling down

In 1014, Anglo-Saxons and Norwegian Vikings attacked the Danish Vikings in London. The Danish Vikings threw spears at them from the old London Bridge.

The attackers used roofs to protect their boats. They tied ropes to the bridge and pulled it down. This led to the song "London Bridge is falling down".

Viking attacks on London ended when Canute became King in 1016. He united the invaders and the Anglo-Saxons. Peace came and London grew wealthy.

Edward's Abbey

God blesses the Abbey.

Edward's funeral procession

Seven years after Canute died, Edward the Confessor became king. He built Westminster Abbey. The Abbey was finished in 1065, just before Edward died.

Edward was buried in the Abbey. The picture above is the oldest picture of the Abbey. It shows the Abbey's completion, its blessing and Edward's burial.

After his death, Edward was made a saint. His Abbey no longer stands, but there is a Westminster Abbey on the site. The Abbey you see today was built by Henry III.

At www.usborne-quicklinks.com you'll find a link to a website all about life in Anglo-Saxon times.

Medieval London

In 1066, after Edward the Confessor's death, William the Conqueror invaded England from France. The centuries from the invasion up until 1485 are known as the medieval period in English history.

Jousts like this one were a popular entertainment on medieval holidays.

The medieval city

Medieval London was much smaller than today's London. The streets would have looked very different, too. The houses were made mainly of wood, and the roads were covered in stones called cobbles. This picture shows how a medieval London street might have looked.

Houses were heated by fires, with chimneys to let out the smoke.

Shops had signs with pictures to show what they sold, because most people couldn't read.

You could buy food such as pies, fruit and spiced meat in the street.

Merchants and craftsmen

There were many merchants and craftsmen. Streets were named after them, for example, bread was sold on Bread Street. Merchants and craftsmen joined together to form powerful groups called Guilds, which still exist today. Each Guild had a coat-of-arms like the one above.

The Blacksmiths' coat-of-arms

At www.usborne-quicklinks.com you'll find a link to a website where you can explore animated scenes of medieval London.

Upper floors stuck out over the street.

7

Tudor and Elizabethan London

Henry VIII

Henry VII became king in 1485, followed by Henry VIII. They were the first Tudor kings (Tudor was their family name). Henry VIII's daughter, Elizabeth I, was the last Tudor; the time when she was queen is called the Elizabethan period. Under the Tudors, London grew wealthier and bigger, spreading beyond the old City walls. By 1600, it had a population of about 200,000 people.

The copy of the Golden Hinde at sea

Elizabethan theatres and Shakespeare's Globe

The first London theatres were built in Elizabethan times. The Globe Theatre was the most famous. Shakespeare owned part of the Globe and his plays were performed there.

The modern Globe opened in 1997.

A copy of the Globe has been built by the Thames. There are performances of Shakespeare's plays here in the summer. You can go on tours around it and see an exhibition about its history.

Ships and boats

The Tudors built lots of ships, including magnificent sailing ships, or "galleons", like the Golden Hinde. You can visit a copy of the Golden Hinde, a famous Elizabethan galleon, which is moored at Saint Mary Overie Dock in London. Some Tudor ships left London to explore new parts of the world, such as America and India. The best way to travel around Tudor London was by boat along the Thames. You can still travel up and down the Thames by boat today, although modern boats look rather different from Tudor ones.

The picture below shows what an Elizabethan theatre looked like inside.

Wealthy people could watch from seats in the galleries.

The theatre was built in a ring. It had no roof in the middle.

The stage stuck out into the middle of the theatre.

It was cheapest to stand in front of the stage and watch. People who stood here were called "groundlings".

At **www.usborne-quicklinks.com** you'll find links to websites where you can plan a Tudor sea voyage and tour the Globe theatre.

Death and disaster

Black rats carried fleas that spread a deadly plague.

After Elizabeth I died, James I became king. He was the first Stuart king, followed by Charles I. During the time of the Stuarts, there was a civil war and London was hit by disasters. In 1665, plague killed thousands of Londoners, and in 1666, fire destroyed much of the city. Historians know a lot about Stuart London because a man called Samuel Pepys wrote about it in his diaries.

The Monument was built in memory of the Great Fire.

Civil war

In the 1640s, civil war broke out between King Charles I and Parliament. The king lost and he was executed in London. His son later became King Charles II.

Plague

In 1665, plague killed about 100,000 people in London – one in three of those who stayed in the city. Many people escaped to the countryside.

Plague was spread by fleas carried by black rats from ships. People with plague were shut in their houses. Their doors were marked with warning crosses.

Nobody knew how to cure plague. People who caught it got black marks on their skin and soon died. Their bodies were collected in carts and buried in pits.

The Great Fire of London

In 1666, a huge fire swept across London. It began in a baker's kitchen in Pudding Lane and lasted four days. The fire destroyed four-fifths of the City, including the old Saint Paul's Cathedral, which was later rebuilt by Sir Christopher Wren.

At www.usborne-quicklinks.com you'll find links to websites about the Great Fire, plague and Pepys' eyewitness accounts.

The Great Fire of London destroyed many of the old, wooden buildings in the city, but stone buildings like the Tower of London (shown below) survived.

People tried to escape the fire in boats.

The eighteenth century

In 1714, George I became king. He began a line of kings and queens called the Hanovers, who ruled Britain until 1837. At this time, Britain was one of the most powerful countries in the world, with London at the heart of its trade and art.

A painting of the River Thames by an Italian painter called Canaletto.

London art

Writers, painters and actors gathered in eighteenth-century London. Two painters called Hogarth and Canaletto became famous for painting London scenes.

At www.usborne-quicklinks.com you'll find a link to a website where you can see paintings by Hogarth.

Hogarth in his London studio

Town houses

In the eighteenth century, many new town houses were built. These houses were tall and three windows wide. They had arched doorways, with a window above called a fanlight. You can still see this kind of house today.

Town houses today

Pleasure gardens

In a pleasure garden

Pleasure gardens started to become popular in eighteenth-century London. They were like early amusement parks, with stalls and entertainers to amuse the crowds.

Finance

Business in Exchange Alley

Financial business began to develop in London. A lot of business was done in coffee houses, especially in a street called Exchange Alley (where the Stock Exchange stands today).

River business

Inspectors checking goods

Ships brought goods like coffee and silk to London. The goods were unloaded in the port and checked by inspectors. Some goods were unloaded in secret to avoid inspection.

London life

Thief in a pillory

The streets of London were badly lit and full of beggars and thieves. If thieves were caught, they were put in a "pillory", where people threw things at them. Some thieves were hanged.

Victorian London

In 1837, Victoria became queen at the age of 18. The time while she was queen is called the Victorian era. At this time, London was the heart of a powerful Empire. The city was busy with trade and industry, and it grew fast. Better lighting, plumbing and transport developed, too. By the time Victoria died in 1901, London was a very different city.

Victoria ruled Britain for 64 years – longer than any other king or queen.

Ships on the Thames

The Thames by London Bridge

In Victorian times, the River Thames was crowded with ships. Sailing ships were replaced by new steam-powered ships or "steamers", many of which were built in London. People took trips in "penny steamers" along the river.

Other ships brought goods to London from all over the Empire. Huge new docks were built for them. Nowadays, these docks are used by pleasure boats. The old dock buildings have been turned into offices and apartments.

New buildings

Saint Pancras Station

Much of modern London was built in Victorian times. Hundreds of new homes were built as the city grew. Many grand buildings, such as Saint Pancras Station, date from Victorian times, too.

Slum houses

Poor people often had to live in run down "slum" houses. Children had to make money by begging or sweeping chimneys. In 1870, a law was passed saying all children had to go to school.

At www.usborne-quicklinks.com you'll find links to websites where you can play online games and explore Victorian Britain.

People in a street of slum houses

Railways

A Victorian steam train

The railways changed London forever. Journeys became much quicker, bringing many parts of Britain within reach of the capital. People could live outside London and travel to work in the city by train.

The Underground

An early Underground train

In 1863, the world's first Underground railway opened in London. It was powered by steam and ran between Paddington and Farringdon. This was the start of the Underground system we use today.

A modern Underground sign

The twentieth century

London grew even bigger in the twentieth century. Many more people went to live in the city suburbs and travelled to work by train, bus or car. The city changed too, with new buildings replacing those damaged by bombs during the Second World War.

Early twentieth-century life

The Ritz Hotel opened in 1905.

A London bus around 1910

In the early part of the century, many luxury hotels, theatres and restaurants were built. Big stores like Selfridges and Harrods were popular, too.

Today's transport system began to develop around this time, and motor buses were introduced. You can see early buses in London's Transport Museum.

Second World War destruction

Bomb damage in a London suburb

London was hit by hundreds of bombs during the Second World War. Some of its oldest buildings were badly damaged. After the war, they were repaired or replaced.

The City was completely changed by new buildings.

At www.usborne-quicklinks.com you'll find a link to a website where you can learn about life in London during the bombing.

Swinging sixties and fashion

In the 1960s, British designers like Mary Quant were fashion leaders of the world. London streets like the King's Road and Carnaby Street became famous for their trendy fashion boutiques.

The Mary Quant flower logo
©2001 Mary Quant

Model Jean Shrimpton in a fashionable sixties outfit

Docklands

In the 1980s, the old docks on the Isle of Dogs were transformed by modern high-rise blocks. The new development is called Docklands. The 250m (800ft) tower at One Canada Square is one of the tallest buildings in Britain today. Docklands is linked to the rest of London by a light railway with automatic trains. The railway has good views of the new buildings and the old docks.

The tower at One Canada Square in Docklands

Air travel and London airports

A plane landing at City airport

Later in the twentieth century, air travel became more important. New airports were built to link London with the rest of the world. City airport is the most central. Gatwick and Heathrow are the biggest.

Millennium London

In the new millennium, London continues to grow. It now has a population of over seven million, making it by far the biggest city in Britain.

The arrival of the millennium was marked by the opening of many new attractions and exhibitions, so there is more to see and do in London than ever before.

Millennium Mile

Part of the Millennium Mile

The Millennium Mile is a riverside walk between Westminster Bridge and Tower Bridge. There are lots of things to visit along the way, including the London Eye, the Globe Theatre and the Tate Modern.

30 St Mary Axe

30 St Mary Axe in the City

30 St Mary Axe, also known as the Gherkin, was opened in 2004. It is 180m (590ft) tall and is used for offices. Surprisingly, the only curved piece of glass in it is the cap at the top.

At www.usborne-quicklinks.com you'll find a link to a webcam showing live pictures of the Eye.

London Eye

The London Eye is a giant wheel on the South Bank. At 135m (450ft) high, it is the highest passenger-carrying wheel ever built. It is three times higher than Tower Bridge. You can go on rides on the wheel, which turns slowly to give you spectacular views over the River Thames and central London.

The London Eye towers above the South Bank.

Millennium Bridge

The Millennium Bridge

The Millennium Bridge is the first new bridge to be built in central London for more than 100 years. It links Saint Paul's Cathedral to the Tate Modern.

The Tate Modern

The Tate Modern is a new museum of modern art by the Thames. The building used to be a power station and the tower is the old power station chimney.

Westminster Abbey

$\mathbb{W}$estminster Abbey is one of the oldest buildings in London and one of the most important religious buildings in the country. The first Abbey was founded nearly a thousand years ago by Edward the Confessor. The Abbey was rebuilt between the thirteenth and sixteenth centuries, and this is the Abbey you see today.

Edward the Confessor, who built the first Westminster Abbey

Abbey legend

A legend says that Saint Peter came in a boat to bless a church on the Abbey site. On the way, he helped the boatman to catch lots of fish.

Abbey monks

For centuries, monks lived in the Abbey and farmed the fields around it. You can still see the monks' cloisters (covered walks) and a garden where herbs still grow.

Thorney Marsh

The first Abbey was built on an island in an area called Thorney Marsh. Over time, this area has been drained so the Abbey is no longer on an island.

Henry's Abbey

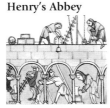

Henry III rebuilt Edward's Abbey in a grand style, with a magnificent chapel dedicated to Edward the Confessor. Henry had to sell his jewels to pay for the building.

The Abbey today

The front of Westminster Abbey as it looks today

Religious services are still held each day in the Abbey. You can look around it between the services. The cut-away picture on the right shows the layout of the Abbey.

At www.usborne-quicklinks.com you'll find links to websites where you can hear Westminster's bells and take an interactive tour.

The Unknown Warrior

The tomb of the Unknown Warrior commemorates British soldiers who died in the First World War. There really is the body of an unknown soldier buried in the tomb.

Tomb of the Unknown Warrior

Nave (main hall)

14

Abbey museum

The Abbey museum has models of historic figures, including Elizabeth of York. The pictures of queens on playing cards are based on her. There are also models of the Crown Jewels, used for rehearsals of the crowning ceremony.

Playing card queens are based on Elizabeth of York.

Saint Edward's Chapel

Edward's tomb

Edward the Confessor was made a saint after he died. He is buried in his own chapel along with nine more English kings and queens, including Henry V. When Henry was buried, his horses were led to the High Altar.

Henry VII's Chapel

Henry VII's Chapel has a grand interior, shown on the right. Many English kings and queens are buried here, including Henry VII, Mary and Elizabeth I. One tomb contains bones that were found in the Tower of London. They are probably the bones of the two young princes who vanished after being locked in the Tower in the fifteenth century.

The interior of Henry VII's Chapel

Saint Edward's Chapel

Henry VII's Chapel

Battle of Britain Memorial Window

Entrance to the Abbey

Choir

High Altar

Tombs of Mary and Elizabeth I

Poets' Corner

Chapter House

Cloisters

Kings and Queens

English kings and queens have been crowned in the Abbey since 1066, when William the Conqueror became king. The present queen, Elizabeth II, was crowned in the Abbey in 1953, by the Archbishop of Canterbury. 8,000 people were at the ceremony and for the first time, millions of people were able to watch on television.

The crowning of Queen Elizabeth II

Coronation Chair

Kings and queens are crowned while sitting on the Coronation Chair, shown above, which is kept in the Abbey.

Shakespeare's memorial

Poets' Corner

In Poets' Corner, you can see memorials to famous writers like Shakespeare. Other parts of the Abbey are set aside for memorials to statesmen, scientists, soldiers, musicians and other people.

The Houses of Parliament

The Houses of Parliament are the home of the British Government. Government business is divided between the two Houses. MPs, or Members of Parliament, are elected to sit in the House of Commons, where new laws are made. The laws are discussed and amended in the Upper House. You can go in the buildings, if you make arrangements.

Medieval Palace

The Parliament buildings are called the Palace of Westminster. The Palace dates from medieval times. In 1834, a fire destroyed most of the old Palace. Sir Charles Barry rebuilt it in a medieval style called Gothic.

Guy Fawkes

On November 4, 1605, a man called Guy Fawkes was found in a Palace cellar. He was about to set fire to some barrels of gunpowder. His capture is celebrated with bonfires and fireworks every year on November 5.

Charles I

In 1642, Charles I went to the House of Commons to arrest five MPs who had criticized him. The MPs escaped. Since then, the king or queen has been forbidden to enter the House of Commons.

State Opening

The State Opening is held each year in November. The king or queen makes a speech from a throne in the Upper House. A man called Black Rod summons MPs from the Commons to hear the speech.

The Houses of Parliament from Parliament Street

The intricate stone carvings were designed by Augustus Pugin.

The Clock Tower is often called Big Ben.

Inside the Palace

The Palace of Westminster has over 1,000 rooms and 3km (2 miles) of corridors.

Victoria Tower

Millions of government documents are kept here, including copies of every law passed by Parliament since the 1400s. A flag flies on the Tower when Parliament is sitting during the day.

Central Lobby

The Central Lobby is the main reception area. It is decorated with mosaics. The Speaker (who is in charge of the Commons) walks through here on the way to debates, carrying the Mace, the symbol of royal authority.

The Mace is a huge staff shaped like a club.

Westminster Hall

Westminster Hall is one of the few remaining parts of the old medieval Palace. The Hall has a huge wooden roof decorated with carved angels. It has been used for Royal banquets and State trials.

Big Ben

Big Ben is the huge bell in the Clock Tower. The bell may have been named after Sir Benjamin Hall, who supervised the rebuilding of Parliament, or after a famous boxer.

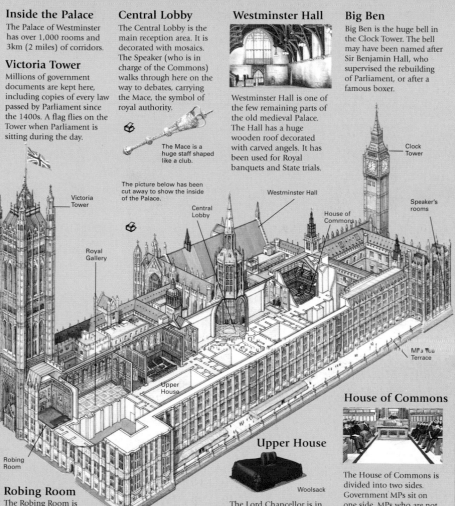

The picture below has been cut away to show the inside of the Palace.

Victoria Tower

Royal Gallery

Central Lobby

Westminster Hall

House of Commons

Clock Tower

Speaker's rooms

MPs Tea Terrace

Upper House

Robing Room

Robing Room

The Robing Room is where the king or queen puts on the Robes of State before opening parliament. The walls are decorated with scenes from the story of King Arthur.

At www.usborne-quicklinks.com you'll find a link to a website with facts and games about Parliament.

Upper House

Woolsack

The Lord Chancellor is in charge of the Upper House. He sits on the Woolsack, which is a big cushion filled with wool. It symbolizes what was once England's main source of wealth.

House of Commons

The House of Commons is divided into two sides. Government MPs sit on one side. MPs who are not part of the Government sit on the other side; they are called the Opposition. The distance between the two sides is the length of two drawn swords.

The City

The City coat-of-arms

The City of London occupies one square mile in the middle of the capital. The City once made up the entire town of London, surrounded by a wall built by the Romans. It is now a modern business district, but you can still see many reminders of its historical past.

A dragon holding the City arms

Bank of England

Gold bars

The Bank of England keeps the British government's money. In its museum, you can see gold bars, and swords and guns once used to defend the bank.

The Bank has vaults full of gold. In the nineteenth century, a workman found a sewer tunnel that led to the vaults. He didn't take any gold but told the Bank about the tunnel, and was rewarded for his honesty.

Guilds and the Guildhall

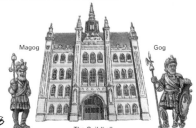

Magog   Gog

The Guildhall

The City Guilds were set up by medieval merchants and craftsmen to look after their trades. The Guilds once controlled all City business, but now they work mainly for charity. The Guildhall is one of the City's oldest buildings. You can see statues of the legendary giants Gog and Magog there.

> At **www.usborne-quicklinks.com** you'll find a link to a website where you can see pictures of the City.

City dragons

A pair of dragons

Statues of dragons holding the City coat-of-arms guard all the main entrances to the City. You can see dragons like this on London Bridge and on Victoria Embankment. There are more dragons on walls and streetlamps around the City.

This picture shows a view over the River Thames towards the City.

Old and new

Although the City is the oldest part of London and has many old buildings, it also has some spectacular new ones.

The Lloyds Building is one of the most dramatic modern buildings in the City. At night, you can see it lit up in blue and green. Saint Bride's is a famous old City church. Its steeple (tower) inspired a baker to make the first tiered wedding cake.

Saint Bride's steeple

The Lloyd's Building

The Monument

The Monument was built in 1677 in memory of the Great Fire of London. It is 62m (202ft) from the shop where the Fire began, and 62m (202ft) high. There is a good view of the City from the top.

The Monument

This is a brass ball covered with brass flames.

Viewing platform

There are 311 stairs inside the Monument which you can climb to the top.

Lord Mayor

The City is governed separately from the rest of London and has its own Lord Mayor. A new Mayor is chosen each year from among the City Guilds. In November, the new Mayor travels through the City in a golden coach, followed by carnival floats. At other times, you can see the coach at the Museum of London. The procession is called the Lord Mayor's Show. It ends with fireworks over the Thames.

The Lord Mayor in his coach

At www.usborne-quicklinks.com you'll find a link to a website describing traditional London events.

Ceremonies held in the City

Many ceremonies are held each year in the City. Most of them date from medieval times. A few ceremonies are listed below.

Knollys rose

In June, the Company of Watermen and Lightermen give the Mayor a rose. The rose was a fine imposed on Lady Knollys in the 1400s.

Boar's head gift

In December, the Butchers' Company gives the Mayor a boar's head on a silver plate. It is payment for land given to them in the 1300s.

Quit rents

Every year, the City pays rent to the king or queen for two properties. The rent is a billhook, a hatchet, six horseshoes and 61 nails.

Saint Paul's Cathedral

Saint Paul's is the cathedral of the City of London. Up to three million people visit Saint Paul's each year, and its dome has become a symbol of London throughout the world. You can read about its history below. The cut-away picture on the right explains some of the features to look out for inside the cathedral.

Saint Paul's dome is a famous London sight.

The ball and cross on top of the dome weigh about seven tonnes.

Old Saint Paul's

Old Saint Paul's was founded in Anglo-Saxon times. Later, it fell into neglect. People took sheep to market through the nave.

The Great Fire

Old Saint Paul's after the fire

Old Saint Paul's was destroyed by the Great Fire of London in 1666. The fire was so hot, it melted the cathedral bells.

Wren and the new Saint Paul's

Sir Christopher Wren

The floor under the dome

After the fire, Sir Christopher Wren designed a new Saint Paul's. There is some Latin writing about Wren on the floor under the dome. It says: "If you seek his monument, look around you."

Wartime

Saint Paul's during the war

During World War Two, a lot of bombs hit the buildings around Saint Paul's, but the cathedral survived.

Saint Paul's today

Saint Paul's is still used for religious ceremonies and special events, like grand weddings. You can visit it when it is not being used.

At www.usborne-quicklinks.com you'll find a link to a website where you can explore Saint Paul's.

Charles and Diana in Saint Paul's

Prince Charles and Lady Diana were married in Saint Paul's in 1981.

The bells

The two bells in the clock tower are called Great Paul and Great Tom. Great Paul is the biggest bell in England. It rings every day at 1pm to let people know it is lunchtime. Great Tom rings when a king or queen dies.

Front entrance

The bells in the other tower are rung on Sundays and special occasions.

The Dome and the Whispering Gallery

The dome of Saint Paul's is 111m (364ft) high. It is actually made of two domes, one inside the other. The inner dome is decorated with pictures of Saint Paul.

The Whispering Gallery runs around the inner dome, 259 steps above the ground. It gets its name because even a whisper can be heard all around it.

Outer dome

Inner dome

Whispering Gallery

Nave

Clock tower

Choir

American Chapel

Duke of Wellington

American Chapel

The American Memorial Chapel is dedicated to Americans who died in the Second World War. Their names are in a list in a glass case. Carvings of American animals decorate the chapel.

The Choir

The choir mosaics

The ceiling of the choir is covered with pictures called mosaics, made up of thousands of tiny bits of glass. The mosaics show angels, animals and birds.

Wooden carvings

The choir has wooden stalls carved by a craftsman called Grinling Gibbons. A modern craftsman works full-time restoring the carvings. You can spot new carvings because the wood is lighter.

The Nave

The main hall is called the nave. On one side of the nave, there is a huge monument to the Duke of Wellington. On the top, there is a statue of the Duke on his horse, Copenhagen.

The Crypt

A crypt (cellar) runs under the whole cathedral. Many famous people are buried down here, including Wren, the Duke of Wellington and Admiral Lord Nelson.

Tower of London

The Tower of London was started by William the Conqueror in 1078. More buildings have been added over the centuries. William built the Tower as a castle and a palace. Since then, it has been used as a zoo and a mint (where money is made), as well as to store weapons. It is most famous, however, as a prison.

The Tower guards are called Beefeaters. They wear Tudor-style uniforms of red or blue.

The Orb and Saint Edward's Crown, some of the Crown Jewels kept at the Tower

The White Tower

The White Tower. This tower got its name in the thirteenth century, when it was painted with whitewash.

The White Tower is at the heart of the Tower of London site. More than 900 years old, it is the oldest building on the site. The White Tower has been home to kings and queens, as well as their prisoners. The first prisoner ever held in the White Tower escaped by climbing down a rope that had been hidden inside in a wine barrel.

Armoury

A suit of armour

The Tower Armoury was used to store weapons and armour. You can still see Henry VIII's suits of armour on display there.

A block and axe

Convicted prisoners were executed at the Tower. In the Armoury, you can see a real block and axe once used to execute prisoners.

The Crown Jewels

The Crown Jewels have been kept at the Tower since the fourteenth century. You can see them on display in the Jewel House. The collection includes Saint Edward's Crown, used to crown a new king or queen, and the Imperial State Crown, which has 3,000 precious jewels.

Traitor's Gate

Traitor's Gate leads into the Tower from the river. It got its name because many prisoners brought through it were accused of being traitors. Few of them left the Tower alive.

At www.usborne-quicklinks.com you'll find a link to a website all about the Tower, past and present.

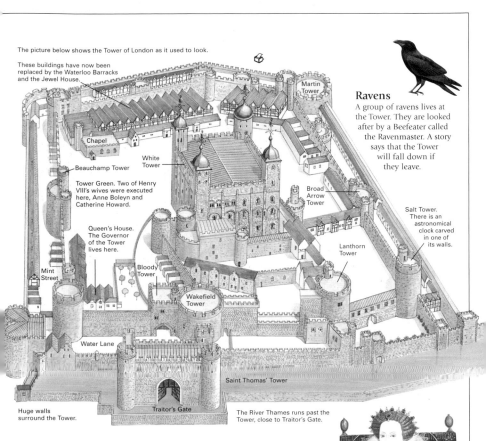

The picture below shows the Tower of London as it used to look.

These buildings have now been replaced by the Waterloo Barracks and the Jewel House.

Martin Tower

Chapel

White Tower

Beauchamp Tower

Tower Green. Two of Henry VIII's wives were executed here, Anne Boleyn and Catherine Howard.

Broad Arrow Tower

Queen's House. The Governor of the Tower lives here.

Salt Tower. There is an astronomical clock carved in one of its walls.

Lanthorn Tower

Mint Street

Bloody Tower

Wakefield Tower

Water Lane

Saint Thomas' Tower

Huge walls surround the Tower.

Traitor's Gate

The River Thames runs past the Tower, close to Traitor's Gate.

Ravens

A group of ravens lives at the Tower. They are looked after by a Beefeater called the Ravenmaster. A story says that the Tower will fall down if they leave.

Famous Tower prisoners

In 1483, the heir to the throne, Prince Edward, and his brother were imprisoned in the Tower by their uncle, who made himself king. The princes disappeared. Over 100 years later, bones thought to be theirs were found in the Tower and buried in Westminster Abbey.

Other famous Tower prisoners have included Anne Boleyn, wife of Henry VIII, Sir Walter Raleigh, the explorer, and Queen Elizabeth I, who was imprisoned by her sister, Queen Mary.

The two young princes, who disappeared after being imprisoned in the Tower.

Elizabeth I was imprisoned in the Tower before she became queen.

The River Thames

London became an important city because of the River Thames. In the nineteenth century, London was one of the busiest ports in the world and the river was crowded with ships. Now, though, the river is mainly used by pleasure boats.

At **www.usborne-quicklinks.com** you'll find a link to a website where you can discover more things to do on the River Thames.

London Bridge

Old London Bridge had a series of stone arches with a street of houses along the top.

This picture of London Bridge is based on a seventeenth century engraving by John Visscher.

Traitors' heads were displayed on the bridge.

The first London Bridge was built by the Romans. It was made of wood. In the twelfth century, it was rebuilt in stone.

The old stone bridge became a famous landmark. Until 1750, it was the only bridge over the Thames in London.

The bridge was rebuilt in 1831, and again in 1973; this is the bridge you see today. The 1831 bridge is now in the USA.

River activities, past and present

The river used to flow more slowly and sometimes froze. Frost fairs with puppet shows, stalls and games were held on the ice.

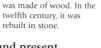

A winner

The umpire

Doggett's Coat and Badge Race dates from 1715. Six boatmen take part, and the winner gets a special coat with a silver badge on it.

In July, cygnets (young swans) on the river are marked with beak nicks to show who owns them. This is called swan-upping.

The Universities of Oxford and Cambridge hold a boat race on the river every Easter. The race is over 6km (4 miles) long.

Tower Bridge

Tower Bridge is the only Thames bridge which opens. The middle of the bridge has two sections (called bascules) that can be raised to let ships through.

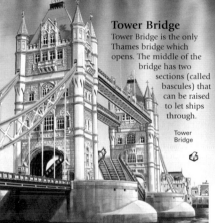

Tower Bridge

Cleopatra's Needle

Cleopatra's Needle is an ancient Egyptian monument. It was brought to London in the 1870s and it now stands on Victoria Embankment by the River Thames. There is a statue of a Sphinx (a mythical Egyptian creature) on each side of it. When Cleopatra's Needle was put up, a box was buried underneath it. Inside the box there are Victorian objects such as newspapers, cigars and pictures of beautiful women.

Cleopatra's Needle

A Sphinx

Galleons and schooners

Elizabethan galleons once sailed on the river. You can visit a full-size replica of one called the Golden Hinde, now a museum.

Schooners used to trade goods around the British coast. You can sometimes see restored schooners on the river today.

Covent Garden

Covent Garden used to be a famous market. For hundreds of years, fruit, flowers and vegetables were sold here. It is still a popular shopping area today, although it now mostly sells clothes and crafts. It has a lively atmosphere, with many theatres, street performers, outdoor cafés and restaurants.

Covent Garden today

Piazza

Market stalls

The first Covent Garden market

Covent Garden was once a convent garden, which is how it got its name. The monks from Westminster Abbey grew vegetables there. They sold some of the vegetables, starting the first Covent Garden market.

The old convent garden

Central Market

In 1830, the Central Market was built. It had several buildings linked together by glass roofs. The Central Market housed the Covent Garden fruit and vegetable market until it moved in the 1970s.

Covent Garden today

You can still shop in Covent Garden today, although there is no longer a fruit and vegetable market. The area is also famous for its theatre associations, which go back to the seventeenth century.

The Royal Opera House

Close by the Central Market, you can see the Royal Opera House, one of the best-known theatres in Covent Garden. It is home to the Royal Opera and Royal Ballet. Some of the most famous singers and dancers in the world have performed here. The building has recently been restored and you can go on tours of it.

The Royal Opera House

Shops and stalls

The Central Market today

After the fruit and vegetable market moved, the old Central Market buildings were restored. Today, they are full of small shops where you can buy everything from pots and pans to toys and clothes. Around the Market, there are many stalls selling crafts such as pottery and knitting. The stalls are set up on Victorian stands from the old flower market.

At **www.usborne-quicklinks.com** you'll find a link to a website with details of what's on at the Royal Opera House.

Street theatre and the Piazza

A Punch and Judy puppet show

In the 1630s, Inigo Jones built the Covent Garden Piazza, surrounded by Italian-style houses. The original houses are no longer there, but you can still see the Piazza, which is famous for street theatre.

The first Punch and Judy show in England was performed in the Piazza in 1662. You can see all kinds of performers in the Piazza today, including jugglers, musicians, mime artists and "living statues".

A living statue in the Piazza

The actors' church

The portico of Saint Paul's

Saint Paul's Church faces onto the Piazza. It is known as the actors' church. It is close to many theatres and there are lots of memorials to actors inside the church. Saint Paul's Church was built by Inigo Jones. It has a grand porch, or "portico". There is a quiet garden, behind the church where you can sit.

Seven Dials

Seven Dials is a junction near Covent Garden where seven streets meet. It was laid out over 300 years ago, and is named after the sundial in the middle. This sundial actually has six faces, not seven, because there were only six streets in the first plans. Seven Dials used to be a slum, but it has now transformed into a fashionable shopping district. It is well-known for its trendy clothes and accessories stores, and famous restaurants and theatres.

The current sundial, an exact replica of the original

The Theatre Royal

The Theatre Royal in Drury Lane is the oldest theatre in Covent Garden and dates back to 1663. It is said to be haunted. In Victorian times, a bricked-up room was found. Inside, there was a skeleton with a dagger in it.

At **www.usborne-quicklinks.com** you'll find links to websites where you can learn more about Covent Garden, past and present.

Neal's Yard

Neal's Yard is tucked away between two of the roads that make up Seven Dials. It is named after the district's designer, Thomas Neale. Neal's Yard is packed with popular cafés and restaurants, and unusual shops selling everything from beads and herbal remedies to skateboarding equipment.

At **www.usborne-quicklinks.com** you'll find a link to a website with an interactive map of the shops in the Seven Dials area.

Some of the shops and cafés in Neal's Yard

Theatre Royal entrance

27

Trafalgar Square

Trafalgar Square used to be the site of the Royal Mews, where hunting falcons were kept. The Square was built in Victorian times. It was named in honour of the British victory, led by Admiral Lord Nelson, at the Battle of Trafalgar in 1805.

The original layout of the Square has not really changed, but it has been added to. The fountains you see today were designed in the 1930s.

This picture shows a view across the Square.

Building Nelson's Column

Workmen eating dinner on top of Nelson's Column

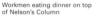

Nelson's statue on display

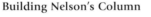

Nelson's Column was built in 1840. It is one of London's most famous landmarks. When it was finished, fourteen workmen ate dinner on top of it.

Nelson's statue has one arm and one eye; Nelson lost the others in battle. The statue was displayed to the public before it was put up. It has never come down since.

The Trafalgar Square lions

One of the lions guarding Nelson's Column

There are four huge, bronze lions around the base of Nelson's Column. They were made out of metal from guns that had been taken from old battleships. They were designed by the famous animal artist, Sir Edwin Landseer, and put up in the Square in 1868.

Nelson's statue at the top of the Column is three times life-size.

Nelson's Column is just over 51.5m (169ft) high from the base to the very top.

Today, Trafalgar Square is a popular meeting place, especially on New Year's Eve, when people gather there to hear Big Ben strike midnight.

At www.usborne-quicklinks.com you'll find links to websites with images and the latest news about events in Trafalgar Square.

Charles I

Charles I

Distances from London are measured from behind this statue of Charles I. The statue was sold for scrap during the Civil War. The man who bought the statue hid it and gave it back later.

National Gallery

The National Gallery houses one of the biggest picture collections in the world.

At www.usborne-quicklinks.com you'll find a link to a website where you can see online pictures from the National Gallery.

Church of Saint Martin-in-the-Fields

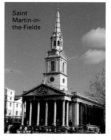

Saint Martin-in-the-Fields

The church of Saint Martin-in-the-Fields is in the north-east corner of the Square. It was built in 1721 and its design inspired many similar churches in America. Concerts are held there.

A brass rubbing

In the crypt (cellar) of Saint Martin-in-the-Fields church, you can make "brass rubbing" pictures like the one above. You can get all the materials you need, for a small charge.

Buckingham Palace

The Queen Victoria Memorial

Buckingham Palace is where the Queen lives. It used to be a town house. John Nash rebuilt it as a palace in the early 1800s. In 1837, Queen Victoria moved in – you can see a memorial to her in front of the Palace. Ever since then, the Palace has been the official home of British kings and queens. Most of the Palace is private, but you can visit the Royal Mews (stables) and the Queen's Gallery. During the summer, you can visit the State Rooms.

Buckingham Palace and the Changing of the Guard

The Changing of the Guard outside Buckingham Palace

The Queen's Household Cavalry at Horse Guards Parade

The different parts of the Palace are described on the next page. Foot Guards guard the Palace. They wear red jackets and tall, furry hats called bearskins.

When Guards come on duty, there is a ceremony called the Changing of the Guard. You can watch it most mornings in front of the Palace.

The Changing of the Guard happens daily in summer, and every other day during the rest of the year. You can also watch a Changing of the Guard ceremony at

Horse Guards Parade, across Saint James's Park from the Palace. The Parade is guarded by mounted Guards from the Queen's Household Cavalry.

The front of Buckingham Palace

North wing

This is where the Queen and Prince Philip have their private rooms. Each morning, a piper plays the bagpipes underneath the Queen's window.

Balcony

This is where the royal family stand to wave to crowds on big occasions. The room behind is decorated in a Chinese style with yellow silk.

Royal flag

When the Queen is at home, you can see her Royal flag flying from the flagpole above the central balcony. This flag is called the Royal Standard.

Post office

The Palace has its own post office. Royal post is sent for free because the British mail is the Royal Mail. You can see the Queen's crest (sign) on mail boxes and vans.

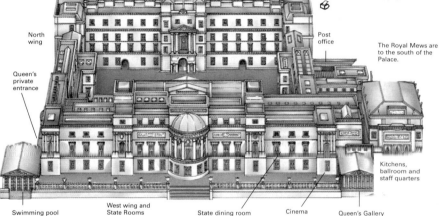

There are about 600 rooms at the Palace, on three main floors.

Central balcony on this side

Flag pole

This picture shows Buckingham Palace from the back, so you can see the State Rooms.

North wing

Post office

The Royal Mews are to the south of the Palace.

Queen's private entrance

Kitchens, ballroom and staff quarters

Swimming pool

West wing and State Rooms

State dining room

Cinema

Queen's Gallery

Royal Mews

The Queen's horses and coaches are kept in the Royal Mews in the Palace grounds. The coaches include the Irish State Coach, shown above.

State Rooms

The west wing contains the grand State Rooms.

At **www.usborne-quicklinks.com** you'll find links to websites about the Queen, members of the royal family and Buckingham Palace.

Queen's Gallery

The Queen's Gallery displays pictures and furniture from the Royal Collection. There are also portraits of royals who have lived at the Palace.

Palace staff

Over 600 people work at the Palace, including cooks, cleaners, plumbers and gardeners. There are even two people who look after the Palace's 300 clocks.

Royal Parks

The Royal Parks are huge parks in the heart of London. They belong to the king or queen, but they are open to everyone during the day. The most central parks are Green Park, Saint James's Park, Regent's Park, Hyde Park and Kensington Gardens. Together, they cover a vast area and make London one of the greenest capital cities in the world.

Around Buckingham Palace

Kensington Gardens • Serpentine • Hyde Park

Buckingham Palace • Green Park • Saint James's Park • The Mall

Saint James's Park and Green Park are on either side of Buckingham Palace. In the picture above, you can see Saint James's Park in front of the tree-lined avenue called the Mall. Green Park is behind the Palace.

Beyond Buckingham Palace in the distance, you can see Hyde Park and Kensington Gardens, separated by a lake called the Serpentine. You can read about these two parks on the next page.

The Parks used to be private royal gardens or hunting forests. Today, they are used by thousands of people. They also provide a haven for wildlife such as birds and squirrels. Some of the birds and squirrels are quite tame and will eat out of your hand.

A grey squirrel

Saint James's Park

Saint James's Park has a large lake with an island in the middle. If you look across the lake, you can see the government offices of Whitehall in the distance. A wide variety of birds live on and around the lake.

The lake in Saint James's Park, looking towards Whitehall

The birds living on the lake include mute swans, geese and Mandarin ducks. There are picture tiles by the lake to help you identify the different birds. You can watch them being fed each afternoon at about 4pm.

A mute swan, one of the many water birds you can see in Saint James's Park

Green Park

Green Park has a grand entrance facing Queen Victoria's memorial outside Buckingham Palace. This entrance is called Canada Gate. There is a memorial to Canadians who died in the two World Wars nearby.

The decorations on Canada Gate, at the entrance to Green Park

Green Park is known for its tree-lined avenues such as the Broad Walk and the Queen's Walk.

At www.usborne-quicklinks.com you'll find a link to a website all about the Royal Parks.

The avenues in Green Park provide a shady place to walk.

Kensington Gardens

Kensington Gardens were created for William III, who lived at Kensington Palace. The Palace is still used by the royal family. You can visit part of it. Diana, Princess of Wales, lived here.

Kensington Palace

In Kensington Gardens, there is a statue of Peter Pan, the famous character from J.M. Barrie's magical story.

At www.usborne-quicklinks.com you'll find a link to the story of Peter Pan.

Peter Pan's statue

The Serpentine and the Long Water

The Serpentine is a popular boating lake.

The Serpentine is a lake which links Hyde Park with Kensington Gardens. The part of it which is in Kensington Gardens is called the Long Water.

You can hire boats and pedaloes on the Serpentine. Some people follow the tradition of swimming in the Serpentine on Christmas Day, however cold it is.

The Diana Memorial Playground

There is a playground dedicated to Diana, Princess of Wales in Kensington Gardens. At the entrance to the playground, you can see the "Elfin Oak", an old tree stump carved with elves and fairies.

Inside the playground, there is a pirate ship to climb over, as well as a mermaid fountain, tepees, a treehouse climbing frame and a garden with musical instruments.

The pirate ship is surrounded by a sandy beach and a paddling pool.

The pirate ship in the Diana Memorial Playground

Hyde Park

In the summer, there are entertainments in Hyde Park, including clowns and puppet shows. Some more events are listed below.

A gun salute

On royal birthdays, you can see gun salutes being fired in Hyde Park. In November, the London to Brighton Veteran Car Run starts from Hyde Park.

A veteran car

Every Sunday in Hyde Park, you can listen to people making speeches at Speakers' Corner. Anyone has the right to speak here, on any subject. The Queen's Household Cavalry ride through Hyde Park every day on their way to Buckingham Palace.

Regent's Park

Regent's Park was designed by John Nash in the 1810s for the Prince Regent (who later became King George IV). Nash also designed the elegant houses you can see surrounding Regent's Park today. On the north side of the park, you will find London Zoo.

One of Nash's houses

Around the Park

There are many things to see in the Park. There is an outdoor theatre, as well as three playgrounds. The Queen Mary Rose Garden is full of flowering plants. Primrose Hill, to the north of the Park, has good views over London.

Regent's Park lake

There is a lake in the Park where you can hire boats. Herons live on one of the islands in the lake.

The bandstand

During the summer, brass bands sometimes play on the bandstand in the Park. You can sit on deckchairs to listen to the music.

Regent's Park has several bridges over its lake and canal.

Regent's Canal

Regent's Canal runs through Regent's Park. The canal was built at the beginning of the nineteenth century so that goods could be transported by boat. You can take boat trips on the canal between Camden Lock and Little Venice.

Canal boats on Regent's Canal

There is a market at Camden Lock that sells clothes, arts and crafts. Every May, there is a procession of decorated boats on the canal.

Richmond Park

There was once a medieval royal palace at Richmond. Although the palace is no longer there, you can still visit Richmond Park, where kings used to hunt deer. The gatehouse of the old palace still stands on Richmond Green.

The White Lodge

Fallow deer

For centuries, Richmond Park was used for hunting. In the Park, there is a small hill called "Henry VIII's mound". It may have been where the king stood to shoot deer.

Henry VIII's mound

In the Park, you can see a building called the White Lodge. The Lodge was built as a hunting lodge for George II. It is now used for ballet lessons by the Royal Ballet School.

About 600 red and fallow deer still live in the Park. If you see the deer in the autumn, it is best to keep away from them as this is when the stags fight each other for mates.

Kew Gardens

The pagoda

As well as being a beautiful place to visit, Kew is an important scientific centre. The Gardens are home to the Royal Botanical Society and house a famous collection of plants and trees from around the world.

Augusta's pagoda

Kew Gardens were started by Princess Augusta. She built the famous Chinese-style pagoda. The pagoda has 10 storeys. You can still see it today in the Gardens.

At www.usborne-quicklinks.com you'll find a link to a website with a virtual tour of Kew Gardens.

Glasshouses

Not all the plants at Kew could grow naturally in Britain. Some of them have to be grown in specially heated glasshouses. Here, you can see exotic plants such as cactuses, giant water lilies and fly-catching plants. The Evolution House shows how plants evolved. Look out for dinosaur footprints among its displays.

Inside the Great Palm House

The Great Palm House is used to grow huge palm trees. The palms produce tropical fruit, including bananas, breadfruit and mangoes. In the basement, there is a marine display with marine plants, fish and coral.

The Great Palm House was built in the 1840s.

Hampton Court

Hampton Court is a grand palace by the River Thames. It was built in the early 1500s for Cardinal Wolsey, who gave it to King Henry VIII. It has been a royal palace ever since. One of the best ways to get there is by boat along the river from Westminster or Richmond.

Hampton Court Palace

Cardinal Wolsey

Wolsey was Henry VIII's chief minister. He lived in luxury at Hampton Court until Henry became angry with him. Wolsey gave Henry the palace to please him. Henry liked the palace, but it didn't help. Wolsey was charged with treason and died. Henry moved to Hampton Court with his second wife, Anne Boleyn. Henry remarried four more times, and brought all his wives here.

Cardinal Wolsey

Things to see

Palace sights include the huge kitchens, where you can see preparations for a feast, and the famous maze in the gardens.

The astronomical clock

On Anne Boleyn's Gate there is an astronomical clock. It shows the time, day, sign of the zodiac and phase of the moon.

The maze is 300 years old.

The Great Hall was used for feasts. It was built for Henry VIII. He was so impatient to finish it that his men worked through the night by candlelight.

The Great Hall

The Haunted Gallery leads to the palace chapel. It is said to be haunted by the ghost of Henry's fifth wife, Catherine Howard. Henry accused her of being unfaithful and she was sentenced to death. She tried to appeal to Henry in the chapel, but only got as far as the gallery before she was carried away screaming. Her ghost is said to appear at night and then, with screams, disappear.

The statues by the Great Gatehouse show the "king's beasts" – animals that represent royalty.

A statue of a dragon, one of the king's beasts

At www.usborne-quicklinks.com you'll find a link to a website all about Hampton Court.

Greenwich

Greenwich is famous for being the centre of the world's time system – time throughout the world is worked out based on "Greenwich Mean Time". Greenwich also has a long sailing history and it is home to the National Maritime Museum and the historic ship, the Cutty Sark.

The Cutty Sark, in dry dock at Greenwich

Royal Observatory

The Royal Observatory is where scientists used to study the sky. You can see their old telescopes, clocks and sundials here.

The Observatory has a special 24-hour clock.

The "Prime Meridian" is the line dividing the world into east and west. It runs through the Observatory, where you can see it marked on the ground. The Meridian is used to work out Greenwich Mean Time, or "GMT".

At **www.usborne-quicklinks.com** you'll find a link to the website of the Royal Observatory.

Maritime Museum

The Museum and Nelson's coat

The National Maritime Museum is about British sailing history. It shows detailed model ships, weapons and uniforms, including the coat Admiral, Lord Nelson was wearing when he was shot at the Battle of Trafalgar in 1805.

At **www.usborne-quicklinks.com** you'll find a link to a website where you can discover the Maritime Museum's different galleries.

Greenwich Park

Greenwich Park is an old royal park with a lake and deer. You get good views of London from the park.

Cutty Sark

You can go round the Cutty Sark, a ship dating from 1869. The Cutty Sark is the last surviving "clipper", or fast sailing ship, (going "at a clip" meant moving fast).

At **www.usborne-quicklinks.com** you'll find a link to a website with pictures of the Cutty Sark.

A display of figureheads from old ships inside the Cutty Sark

Greenwich Market

Greenwich has a busy weekend market. The main covered market sells arts, crafts and toys. Outside, there are more market stalls that sell clothes, books and music.

Thames Barrier

The Thames Barrier, near Greenwich, protects London from floods. It is the world's largest movable flood barrier. When raised, its gates are as high as five-storey houses. You can take boat trips around the barrier. There is also a Visitor Centre where you can see working models of the Barrier.

The Thames Barrier at Woolwich, near Greenwich

British Museum

Front entrance of the British Museum

The British Museum displays historic objects from many cultures, including ancient Egypt, Greece and Roman Britain. It opened in 1759, making it the oldest public museum in the world. Its present building dates from Victorian times, though it was recently extended.

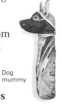

Egyptian mummy

Dog mummy

Egyptian mummies

The British Museum is famous for its Egyptian mummies. The ancient Egyptians thought that life continued after death, so they preserved the body as a mummy for the dead person's spirit to live in. In the museum, you can see mummies of kings and queens and important animals, like cats, dogs and falcons. Mummies were often buried with treasure and household goods to use in the afterlife. Some of these are on display too, along with jars used to store the mummy's insides.

Parthenon Sculptures

Part of the Parthenon Sculptures (or "Elgin Marbles") showing two riders

The Parthenon Sculptures come from the Parthenon temple in Athens. They show the birth of Athena, the goddess of wisdom and war, and processions to honour her. According to legend, Athena was born fully grown out of the head of Zeus.

Rosetta Stone

The Rosetta Stone was the key to understanding the ancient Egyptian picture writing called hieroglyphs. It came from a wall in the village of Rosetta, in Egypt. The writing on the stone tells of ancient battles. The story is repeated in hieroglyphs, in another form of Egyptian and in Greek. By translating the Greek, scholars were able to work out the hieroglyphs.

The Rosetta Stone

Great Court

The Great Court is at the heart of the British Museum. It houses an education centre, café, restaurant, shops and galleries. In the middle of the Court, there is a round building called the Reading Room. The Room is decorated in blue and gold. It contains a library and computers to help you learn about world cultures.

At www.usborne-quicklinks.com you'll find a link to a Web site with a virtual tour of this museum.

The Reading Room in the Great Court of the British Museum

Museum of Childhood

The Bethnal Green Museum of Childhood tells the story of childhood from the sixteenth century to today. It has one of the biggest and oldest collections of toys in the world. As well as toys, you can see children's furniture and clothes, including a complete Victorian girl's wardrobe. There are workshops and events based on the collections, too.

An old dolls' house

An antique train set. Some of the museum's trains are set up so you can watch them running.

Dolls' houses

The museum has many dolls and dolls' houses, from simple cottages to a fully-furnished, Victorian-style mansion. One house is over 300 years old.

Teddies and trains

The museum shows everything from teddy bears to trains, as well as rocking horses, games, puzzles and puppets.

At www.usborne-quicklinks.com you'll find a link to a website about the Museum of Childhood.

A museum teddy bear

Pollock's Toy Museum

A toy theatre

This small museum is packed with toys, including antique dolls and teddy bears, mechanical toys, and different traditional toys from around the world.

Toy theatres

Pollock was famous for making toy theatres, and many old theatres and puppets are on show in the museum.

Space toys

Each museum display contains different kinds of toys. The case on the right is full of space toys.

At www.usborne-quicklinks.com you'll find a link to a website about Pollock's museum.

A display case in Pollock's Toy Museum with space toys, including tin rockets and spaceships, dating back to the 1940s.

Old-fashioned toys from the museum shop, which sells a range of reproduction and pocket-money toys.

Natural History Museum

The Natural History Museum has a huge collection of animals, plants, rocks and fossils. The displays are designed to let you discover things for yourself and have fun with animated exhibits and hands-on activities. The museum has interactive on-line exhibitions, too.

Creepy-crawlies

This gallery is all about creepy-crawlies like insects, spiders and centipedes. You can spot bugs in the kitchen or watch real, live leafcutter ants. Look out for the giant robotic scorpion!

Life Galleries

The Life Galleries start from a huge hall filled with a 26m (85ft) long dinosaur skeleton. The galleries explore life on Earth, covering everything from humans and other mammals to creepy-crawlies and dinosaurs.

At **www.usborne-quicklinks.com** you'll find a link to this museum's website, with online dinosaur activities.

Mammals Gallery

A life-size model of a blue whale, the biggest living animal, hangs from the ceiling of the Mammals Gallery. The model is over 25m (82ft) long, longer than three London buses put together.

Earth Galleries

Dinosaur Gallery

The Dinosaur Gallery is full of life-size dinosaur models. Some of the models are brought to life by robotics, so you can watch dinosaurs move. You can also see real fossils of their bones, teeth and eggs.

From the start of the Earth Galleries, an escalator takes you up through a huge model of planet Earth to more galleries that explore the Earth, the effect we have on it and its place in the universe. You can follow a time-rail back 4,560 million years to the beginning of the Earth, handle rocks and fossils in the Earth Lab, or discover what an earthquake feels like in a special simulator.

Science Museum

The Science Museum is designed to help people understand science both past and present. The displays show everyday machines as well as very advanced ones, from ordinary calculators to real spacecraft.

The marks on the outside of this Apollo 10 Command Module were made by the intense heat as it re-entered the Earth's atmosphere.

Museum machines

You can see all kinds of machines in the museum, including steam engines, ships, cars and planes. There is a whole gallery about flight, which has over 20 aircraft hanging from the roof, including Hurricane and Spitfire fighter planes as well as modern jet planes.

The Wellcome Wing

The displays in this wing are about science today, from genetics to virtual reality. You can watch spectacular science films in the Imax cinema or discover the latest digital technology in Digitopolis. In Digitopolis, you can distort a computer image of your face, or compose your own music.

Inside Digitopolis

Space

This gallery explains all about space travel. Among the exhibits, you can see the Apollo 10 Command Module, which took three astronauts into space in 1969. The Module travelled 800,000km (500,000 miles) in the eight days it was in space.

At **www.usborne-quicklinks.com** you'll find links to websites with online exhibitions and a virtual guide to the Science Museum.

Joining in

The museum is full of things you can join in and do yourself. In Launch Pad, you can send noises across the gallery with a giant sound dish or build a working bridge. In Pattern Pod, you can explore patterns by following footprints or listening to your body sounds.

Pattern Pod at the Science Museum

Things to see and do

Apart from the museums and attractions covered on the previous pages, there are many other things to see and do in London. A few of the most popular ones are shown on these pages.

Madame Tussauds

A wax figure of the actor Johnny Depp as Captain Jack Sparrow

Madame Tussauds is the world's most famous wax museum. Every year, over two million visitors go there to see the lifelike wax figures of famous people. You can see famous actors, models, sports stars, royals and politicians. Famous criminals are kept in the Chamber of Horrors.

At **www.usborne-quicklinks.com** you'll find a link to a website which reveals the secrets behind the wax figures at Tussauds.

Emirates Stadium

The Emirates Stadium is home to Arsenal Football Club, one of the top football teams in England. The stadium tour lets you glimpse life behind the scenes, including the players' changing rooms, the tunnel leading onto the pitch and the coach's seat. There is also a museum of Arsenal's history, where exhibits include boots and shirts worn by famous players.

The Emirates Stadium

At **www.usborne-quicklinks.com** you'll find a link to a website where you can find out more about Arsenal Football Club.

The Stardome at Madame Tussauds

Britain at War

One of the gas masks on display at the Britain at War Experience

Winston Churchill's Britain at War Experience gives a taster of life in London during the Second World War. You can hear the air raid warning siren, visit a shelter, and look at real bombs, ration books, gas masks and photographs. Learn about the role of the Land Girls and what it was like to be evacuated.

At **www.usborne-quicklinks.com** you'll find a link to a website about the Britain at War Experience.

BBC Backstage

The BBC offers a backstage tour which takes you behind the scenes at the Television Centre. Visit a studio or take a look inside the BBC News Centre.

At **www.usborne-quicklinks.com** you'll find a link to a website with details about getting tickets for BBC TV and radio shows.

On the BBC Backstage Tour

City farms

There are several city farms around London. (See a list of them all on pages 60-61.) You can visit them to look at the animals and see how a farm runs. Sometimes, you can help with the farm work.

At **www.usborne-quicklinks.com** you'll find a link to a website where you can meet some city animals.

Pigs on a city farm

HMS Belfast

HMS Belfast is a cruiser dating from 1938. It was used by the British Navy during the Second World War. It is now moored permanently in London and is open as a museum.

HMS Belfast

You can explore all over the ship, from the engine rooms at the bottom to the gun turrets and the Captain's Bridge at the top.

At **www.usborne-quicklinks.com** you'll find a link to a website where you can follow a tour of the ship.

London Dungeon

The London Dungeon has scary displays about crime, torture and executions. Watch out for the spitting gargoyles! You can see wax figures of famous criminals or take a "Judgement Day" boat ride through a replica Traitor's Gate.

The "Judgement Day" ride at the London Dungeon

IMAX cinema

The IMAX cinema near Waterloo Station has the largest cinema screen in Britain. The screen is the height of a ten-storey building. It shows spectacular films, many with special 3D effects.

At **www.usborne-quicklinks.com** you'll find a link to a website with showing times for the IMAX.

The IMAX cinema

Air Force Museum

The Royal Air Force Museum tells the story of flight with over 70 real planes, including Spitfire and Hurricane fighter planes and a Vulcan bomber. You can even try flying a plane yourself in the Tornado flight simulator.

At **www.usborne-quicklinks.com** you'll find a link to a website where you can browse the RAF Museum aircraft collections online.

Butterfly House

The London Butterfly House has hundreds of free-flying butterflies. Tropical butterflies live in a huge glasshouse. British ones live in an outside garden. The insect gallery has insects, lizards and giant spiders.

Holly blue butterfly

Peacock butterfly

Two British butterflies

One of the displays inside the Royal Air Force Museum at Hendon

This plane is a Harrier Jump Jet.

Royal Albert Hall

Royal Albert Hall

The Royal Albert Hall is an oval concert hall. It is famous for the "Proms", held every summer, when you can buy cheap standing tickets to hear classical music.

The IMAX building is surrounded by a curved glass wall.

Alexandra Palace

Alexandra Palace is a grand Victorian building set in a large park. You can tour the palace or visit the park, which has a playground, boating lake, animal enclosure and conservation area. There is also an ice rink and a funfair.

Chessington

On the outskirts of London, Chessington World of Adventures is an amusement park with lots of thrilling rides, live shows and a zoo.

At **www.usborne-quicklinks.com** you'll find a link to a website where you can check out the latest attractions at Chessington.

Dragon Falls at Chessington

At **www.usborne-quicklinks.com** you'll find links to websites where you can find fun online guides to London for children.

More museums

There are many museums in London, devoted to different subjects. As well as the museums already described, the museums on this page are well worth a visit.

The Lord Mayor's Coach

Victoria and Albert Museum

The Victoria and Albert Museum, known as the V&A, displays art and design, including furniture, clothes, jewellery and pottery. There are statues, paintings and photographs, too, including a special collection of miniature portraits. The museum runs tours and story sessions, as well as drama and craft activities like puppet theatre and jewellery-making.

Tipu's Tiger is a famous exhibit in the V&A. It is made of painted wood and shows a tiger attacking a soldier. The tiger can actually growl and roar.

Tipu's Tiger, in the V&A

At **www.usborne-quicklinks.com** you'll find a link to a website where you can see what's on at the V&A.

Museum of London

The Museum of London tells the story of London. There are real Viking and Roman remains, and a treasure trove of Elizabethan jewellery. Look out for the red and gold Lord Mayor's coach. You can visit an eighteenth-century prison cell or Victorian shops.

A piece of Elizabethan jewellery

At **www.usborne-quicklinks.com** you'll find a link to a website where you can uncover the history of London through words, images and sounds.

The outside of the Victoria and Albert Museum

Imperial War Museum

The Imperial War Museum is about war in the twentieth century. It has displays of guns, tanks and planes. You can walk through a soldiers' trench or a bomb-hit London street, or find out about the secret world of spies. One gallery is dedicated to the Holocaust and the people who were killed in it.

At **www.usborne-quicklinks.com** you'll find a link to a website displaying the Imperial War Museum's online exhibitions.

The huge guns outside the front of the Imperial War Museum

London Aquarium

The London Aquarium has displays of fish and sea life from around the world. The biggest tanks are two floors deep and recreate the oceans.

Inside the Aquarium

Watch out for the sharks and piranhas! The rays, starfish and anemones are more friendly. Some of them live in shallow pools where you can stroke them. Video displays tell you more about the fish and how they live.

Porkfish from the London Aquarium

At **www.usborne-quicklinks.com** you'll find a link to a website where you can learn more about the exhibits and even adopt a fish!

Watching sharks at the Aquarium

Stroking friendly sea creatures

London Zoo

London Zoo, started in 1828, is one of the oldest and most famous zoos in the world. It has all sorts of animals and birds, as well as animal rides, talks and displays.

At **www.usborne-quicklinks.com** you'll find a link to a website with a calendar of Zoo events.

Meet the B.U.G.S!

Bear mountain

Sloth bear

One of the biggest enclosures at the Zoo contains a whole "mountain" that was built for the bears to live on.

Rare tigers

There are more than 8,000 animals in the Zoo today, including some very rare animals such as the Sumatran tiger shown below. The Zoo helps to protect rare species by breeding them in captivity, so they don't die out.

Feeding time

Every day you can watch animals such as penguins and pigs being fed (and you can help feed the pigs). The elephants eat the most food.

Blackfooted penguin

The B.U.G.S! exhibition is all about the huge variety of life on Earth, from leafcutter ants to giant anteaters. It explains the threats faced by different animals and plants, and how we can protect them.

A leafcutter ant in the B.U.G.S! exhibit

At **www.usborne-quicklinks.com** you'll find a link to a website where you can find out more about the animals at London Zoo.

Sumatran tiger

Art galleries

London is famous as a centre for arts and culture, and you can see all kinds of art in the city. London art galleries show everything from traditional paintings to precious crafts and strange modern sculptures. You can read about a few of the most famous galleries on this page, and find out about some of the activities they run.

Somerset House, Gilbert Collection and Courtauld Gallery

Somerset House is a grand, eighteenth-century building overlooking the River Thames. It has a huge courtyard that is used for concerts. There are tours, workshops and storytelling sessions, too.

At **www.usborne-quicklinks.com** you'll find a link to a website where you can see historic pictures of Somerset House.

Somerset House is home to the Gilbert Collection and the Courtauld Gallery. In the Gilbert Collection, you can see elaborate gold and silver dishes and mosaics (pictures made of pieces of glass or precious stones).

The fountains in the courtyard of Somerset House

The Courtauld Gallery shows paintings, including many famous paintings from the nineteenth century.

A painting by Degas from the Courtauld Gallery

National Gallery

Detail of a painting by Rousseau at the National Gallery

The National Gallery has a huge collection of pictures, some over 700 years old.

At **www.usborne-quicklinks.com** you'll find a link to a website where you can see some of the National Gallery's famous pictures.

Tate Britain

Tate Britain shows historic British art. You can explore the gallery by following picture trails. At weekends and holidays, there are games and art activities.

Tate Modern

Tate Modern has displays of modern art from around the world. There are tours and workshops, too.

At **www.usborne-quicklinks.com** you'll find a link to a website where you can browse the collections of both Tate galleries.

Theatres

You can see all kinds of shows in London, from Shakespeare's plays to puppet shows and modern musicals. On this page, you can find out about some of the best-known London theatres and the special events they organize.

The National Theatre at night

Pantomimes

At Christmas, many London theatres put on pantomimes (plays based on fairytales). They are performed by famous stars, and the audience is often asked to join in. Traditional pantomimes include the story of Dick Whittington and his cat, as well as fairytales like Cinderella, Snow White, and Aladdin and his magic Lamp.

Pantomime "dames" – female characters played by men dressed up as women

National Theatre

The National Theatre is on the South Bank. It is actually several theatres, so there is always a choice of plays to see. The National also runs backstage trips and theatre workshops.

Royal Shakespeare Company

The Royal Shakespeare Company, or "RSC", puts on plays by Shakespeare and other playwrights at the Barbican. As well as watching the plays, you can go on backstage trips.

The Royal Shakespeare Company logo

The West End

There are so many theatres in London's West End that this area is called "Theatreland". Here, you can see many famous plays, as well as musicals with amazing costumes and special effects.

Idina Menzel playing a witch in the West End musical "Wicked"

Children's theatres in London

Puppets at the Little Angel Theatre

The Little Angel Theatre puts on a wide range of shows using all kinds of puppets. Many of the shows have live music.

The Polka Children's Theatre has puppet and magic shows, as well as music, clowning and stories.

At www.usborne-quicklinks.com you'll find a link to a website where you can tour the Polka Theatre.

The Unicorn Theatre for Children puts on plays full of adventure, magic and comedy. There are theatre workshops, where you act and paint scenery.

Theatre listings

At www.usborne-quicklinks.com you'll find links to websites where you can find the latest theatre listings for children, read fascinating theatre facts and see reviews by children.

Traditions and festivals

There are many regular London traditions and festivals. These include formal State ceremonies and processions, and religious services. Some ancient British traditions are still celebrated too, as well as festivals from other parts of the world.

Trooping the Colour on the Queen's official birthday

Changing the Guard

At 10.30am each day, the Queen's Guards ride through Hyde Park to Horse Guards' Arch, where they go on duty at 11am.

Beating retreat

In May or June, military bands "beat retreat" on Horse Guards Parade. There is a procession with horses carrying big, silver drums.

Beating retreat originally meant beating drums to tell soldiers to go back to their quarters.

Trooping the Colour

This ceremony celebrates the Queen's official birthday in June. The Queen leads a procession to Horse Guards Parade, where the Colour is trooped. This means that the Colour (regimental flag) is carried for everyone to see what it looks like. The ceremony dates back to the eighteenth century.

At **www.usborne-quicklinks.com** you'll find a link to a website where you can learn more about Trooping the Colour.

Pearly Festival

In October, a Pearly harvest festival is held at Saint Martin-in-the-Fields. You can find out about Pearly families on page 50.

Beating the bounds

People once learned village boundaries by going on a procession called "beating the bounds". Every third year in June, the old boundaries around the Tower of London are still beaten. There is a big procession and at every boundary mark, the Chief Warder shouts out "Whack it boys, whack it!" The children in the procession then beat the mark with wooden sticks.

Children beating the bounds

A group of Pearly families

Chinese New Year

A dancer with a lion costume at Chinese New Year

Chinese New Year can fall in January or February, because it depends on the moon. The streets in London's Chinatown are brightly decorated and there is a lively procession to scare away evil spirits. The procession is led by dancers in a lion costume. Red packets of money are hung outside houses to attract the lion and bring good luck.

Notting Hill Carnival

A dancer at the Notting Hill Carnival

In August, there is a Caribbean-style carnival in Notting Hill. People dress up in spectacular costumes and dance in the streets. There is a procession of decorated floats, as well as music from reggae groups and steel bands. The carnival lasts for a weekend, with a children's procession on the Sunday.

At **www.usborne-quicklinks.com** you'll find a link to a website where you can join in the excitement of the Notting Hill Carnival.

Fireworks on
Guy Fawkes' Night

Guy Fawkes' Night

Every November 5, people celebrate the discovery of Guy Fawkes' plot to blow up Parliament. There are bonfires and firework displays in and around London, like the ones shown on this page.

There is an old rhyme about Guy Fawkes' Night which goes:
Remember, remember,
the fifth of November,
Gunpowder treason
and plot.
I see no reason why
gunpowder treason,
Should ever be forgot.

A Guy Fawkes' Night bonfire

Christmas

The Christmas tree in Trafalgar Square

There are lots of Christmas celebrations in London. Each December, the city of Oslo in Norway sends Britain a huge Christmas tree as thanks for wartime help. It is put up in Trafalgar Square and carols are sung around it.

London people

Some London people stand out because they wear special clothes or uniforms. Look out for them as you walk round London. Some famous London people are described on the next page. You can visit the places associated with them.

London police

The Metropolitan Police patrol London. They wear blue uniforms. Some wear tall helmets developed from top hats. The City of London has its own police with different uniforms. The Thames police patrol the river in boats. They have a floating police station by Waterloo Bridge. Mounted police ride through London on horses. The police are nicknamed "bobbies" after Sir Robert (or "Bobby") Peel, the founder of the Metropolitan Police.

A London policeman

A Foot Guard on sentry duty

Foot Guards

Foot Guards guard the Royal palaces. They wear red jackets and tall hats called bearskins.

At www.usborne-quicklinks.com you'll find a link to a website where you can learn more about the role of Foot Guards.

Doormen

Doormen stand outside some hotels. They wear splendid, old-fashioned uniforms.

Chelsea Pensioners

Chelsea Pensioners are old soldiers who wear red uniforms with black hats.

Judges

Judges wear wigs and knee breeches in the style of the eighteenth century.

Pearly Kings

The Pearly Kings were the leaders of the Victorian "costermongers", or street sellers. They got their name because they wore "pearl" buttons on their hats as a sign of authority. Later, they began to wear clothes covered all over in buttons.

The title of Pearly King passes from father to son, and there are Pearly Queens, Princes and Princesses, too. They are now a famous London tradition and do a lot of work for charity.

Doorman at the Lloyds Building

Cockney slang

The costermongers developed the famous cockney slang, where words are replaced with rhyming phrases. You may still hear cockney slang used today.

Loaf of bread = head
Mince pies = eyes
Hampstead Heath = teeth
Daisy roots = boots
North and south = mouth
Rosie Lee = tea

Pat and Carole Jolly, the Pearly King and Queen of Crystal Palace in South London

50

Virginia
Stephen
(VIRGINIA WOOLF)
1882 - 1941
Novelist and Critic
lived here
1907-1911

This plaque is displayed on the house where Virginia Woolf lived.

Commemorative plaques are displayed on hundreds of London houses where famous people lived. They are mostly blue with white lettering.

Dickens House Museum

Charles Dickens

Charles Dickens was a famous Victorian writer. He lived in London and often describes London places in his books. You can visit his old home on Doughty Street in Bloomsbury, which is now a museum.

At www.usborne-quicklinks.com you'll find links to websites with maps and games about Dickens and London.

Dick Whittington

The story of Dick Whittington is a well-known London legend. The story goes that Dick was a poor country boy who came to London to make his fortune, carrying his belongings in a bundle on the end of a stick.

Dick got a job helping a cook. He bought a cat to get rid of the mice in the house. The cook treated him badly and he left. He was on his way home when he heard the Bow bells. The bells said: "Turn again Dick Whittington, Three times Lord Mayor of London", so he turned back.

Meanwhile, Dick's cat had gone onto a ship and was taken to a distant country. The country was troubled by rats, but the cat caught them all. The Emperor of the country gave Dick a fortune in return for the cat. Dick became a wealthy merchant and was Lord Mayor of London three times.

There was a real Dick Whittington who came to London and became a merchant. He owned ships called "cats", and that may be where the story about the cat comes from. The real Dick was Lord Mayor three times in the early 1400s.

You can see a statue of Dick Whittington's cat in Highgate. The Bow bells belong to Saint Mary-le-Bow church in the City.

Statue of Whittington's cat on Highgate Hill

Sherlock Holmes

The famous detective Sherlock Holmes appears in stories by Sir Arthur Conan Doyle. Many of the stories are set in London. Holmes was supposed to live at 221B Baker Street, between 1881 and 1904. This address is now a Sherlock Holmes Museum.

Sherlock Holmes Museum on Baker Street

Winston Churchill

Sir Winston Churchill was Prime Minister of Britain during the Second World War. There is a statue of him near the Houses of Parliament. You can visit the Cabinet War Rooms in Whitehall, his secret headquarters in London during the war.

At www.usborne-quicklinks.com you'll find a link to a website where you can discover more secrets about the War Rooms.

The picture on the left shows a model of Sir Winston Churchill in the Cabinet War Rooms.

Shopping

You can buy almost anything in London. There are thousands of shops and many markets. These pages show just a few of the best-known places to go shopping.

Most big shops stay open until about 7pm from Monday to Saturday, but shut early on Sundays. Markets finish earlier than shops, and may not run every day.

Harrods department store

Harrods first opened in Knightsbridge in 1849. With over a million square feet of shop space, it is one of the largest department stores in Europe. Their motto is 'Everything for Everybody Everywhere'.

At night, Harrods is lit up by over 11,000 light bulbs.

A food hall in Harrods

Luxury stores

Fortnum and Mason sells luxury food. It has a clock with figures of Mr Fortnum and Mr Mason, who come out and bow on the hour.

The Fortnum and Mason clock

Liberty is famous for selling beautiful fabrics. The shop looks like a Tudor house and has an elaborate clock outside.

Hamleys is London's largest toy shop. It has six floors filled with all kinds of toys, from dolls and teddy bears to models, mechanical toys and robots.

The West End, Oxford Street and Regent Street

The West End is one of London's busiest shopping areas. Each year, millions of people shop here. Some nights, there is "late-night" shopping in the West End, when the shops stay open later than usual.

Oxford Street and Regent Street are two famous West End shopping streets. They have lots of department stores and clothes shops. There are big music shops, bookshops, and Disney and Warner Brothers Stores, too.

Oxford Street and Regent Street are decorated with Christmas lights each year. The lights are turned on with a special ceremony in mid-November.

Christmas lights on Oxford Street. The lights are different each year.

A display of toys in Hamleys

At www.usborne-quicklinks.com you'll find a link to a website where you can get up to date with London shopping trends.

Markets

London markets sell all kinds of things, from fruit and vegetables to antiques, crafts and clothes. This page describes a few of the main markets in London.

About 5 million people visit Camden Market each year, making it one of the busiest markets anywhere. It is really several markets, including Camden Lock Market, Canal Market and Stables Market. They sell antiques, jewellery, crafts and clothes.

Camden Lock Market seen from across the canal. There are cafés and shops along the banks of the canal, too.

Greenwich Market, like Camden Market, is really several markets where you can buy new and second-hand clothes, gifts, crafts and antiques.

Covent Garden Market has stalls selling clothes, crafts and jewellery.

Leadenhall Market is a Victorian covered market. It sells meat and fish.

Portobello Road Market is a huge street market with over 2,000 stalls. It sells antiques and old clothes.

Berwick Street Market is a lively market in the heart of Soho. It sells flowers, fruit and vegetables.

Petticoat Lane Market got its name in the 1600s, when clothes sellers gathered there. It still sells clothes and shoes.

One of the stalls at Portobello Road Market

Leadenhall Market

Old Spitalfields Market has lots of small shops and stalls. It sells clothes, arts and crafts. There are also cafés selling food from around the world.

Columbia Road Flower Market comes alive early Sunday morning, selling plants, flowers and gardening equipment.

Brixton Market sells West Indian food including unusual Caribbean fruit and vegetables.

At **www.usborne-quicklinks.com** you'll find links to websites about the different London street markets, with pictures too.

Wholesale markets

Wholesale markets sell goods to traders. They are interesting to visit, but you can't buy in small amounts. They usually finish by 9am.

New Covent Garden Market sells fruits, vegetables and flowers. Billingsgate Market sells fish and Smithfield Market sells meat.

Some workers at Billingsgate wear special hats so they can carry boxes on their heads.

Getting around

An Underground sign

L ondon has the largest public transport network in the world. On average each day, London buses and Underground trains carry about 6.5 million people and travel over 800,000km (497,000 miles). Many people use taxi cabs and overground trains, too.

The London Underground

The London Underground is the oldest in the world. The first trains were steam trains and they ran on the Metropolitan line in 1863. The London Underground is nicknamed the "Tube". About 2.5 million people use it every day. Although it is called the Underground, almost half the system is above ground.

There are over 270 Underground stations in London. This picture shows Canary Wharf, one of the most modern stations.

London Docklands

The Docklands Light Railway connects the Docklands area in east London to the rest of the transport network.

This train is part of the Docklands Light Railway.

London buses

The first London bus started in 1829. It was pulled by horses and it was called an "omnibus", meaning "for all". It took passengers between Paddington and the City.

The first omnibus

Motor buses began in the early 1900s. Nowadays, there are about 700 different bus routes around London. About four million people use London buses each day.

An early motor bus

In the First World War, London buses took soldiers to the battlefront. You can see one, nicknamed "Ole Bill", at the Imperial War Museum. During the war, the bus was painted khaki.

At www.usborne-quicklinks.com you'll find links to websites where you can print out maps of the London Underground (or "Tube"), play a game and plan your journey online.

You can pick up free bus maps from libraries and tourist information centres.

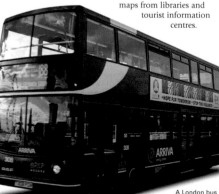
A London bus

Buying tickets

London's public transport system is divided into zones. The cost of a ticket depends on the zones you travel through.

You buy tickets from machines or ticket offices in Underground stations. Travelcards offer unlimited Underground and bus travel. For a small deposit, you can buy an Oyster card and then pay money onto it. Oyster cards offer cheaper fares on buses and the Underground.

If you need a single bus ticket, you can usually buy one from a machine at the bus stop. If there is no machine, you can pay the driver instead.

At www.usborne-quicklinks.com you'll find a link to a website where you can find out about the London Transport Museum.

Railways

Overground trains link London to the suburbs and the rest of Britain, as well as to Europe via the Channel Tunnel. There are 12 main London stations, each serving a particular part of Britain. The main stations have travel centres where you can get travel information and buy tickets.

At **www.usborne-quicklinks.com** you'll find a link to a website where you can check the details of train journeys.

High-speed Eurostar trains connect London, Brussels and Paris.

Taxi cabs

London taxi cabs are usually black, sometimes decorated with advertisements. All taxi cabs have a sign saying "TAXI" on top. When they are free, the sign is lit up. The word "cab" comes from "cabriolet", a kind of horse-drawn carriage once used in London. Today's taxi cabs are large cars that take up to five passengers in the back. Taxi cab drivers have to learn hundreds of special routes. Then, they have to pass a test called "The Knowledge" before they can work as a taxi cab driver.

A London taxi cab

Airports

There are several airports in the London area, but Heathrow and Gatwick are the biggest and the busiest. Both have viewing decks where you can watch planes taking off and landing.

Planes at Heathrow Airport

London's Transport Museum

London's Transport Museum tells the story of transport in London from the nineteenth century. It explores the effect of public transport on the growth of London and on the lives of people living in London. There are real buses and trains, as well as photographs and videos. You can even try driving a bus or a train in special simulators.

Inside London's Transport Museum

Map of central London

This map of central London shows roughly where to find some of the things listed in this book. It also shows some of the major roads to look out for when you are travelling from place to place. There is more detailed information on how to get to all the places listed in this book on the next few pages.

N

MARYLEBONE ROAD

EDGWARE ROAD

BAKER STREET

EUSTON ROAD

TOTTENHAM COURT ROAD

BAYSWATER ROAD

OXFORD STREET

PARK LANE

REGENT STREET

PICCADILLY

KNIGHTSBRIDGE

HYDE PARK CORNER

TRAFALGAR SQUARE

THE STRAND

THE MALL

VICTORIA EMBANKMENT

WHITEHALL

BIRDCAGE WALK

BROMPTON ROAD

SLOANE STREET

BUCKINGHAM PALACE ROAD

VICTORIA STREET

WESTMINSTER

WARWICK ROAD

KINGS ROAD

Kew Gardens and Richmond Park are to the south-west of this map, by the River Thames.

CHEYNE WALK

CHELSEA EMBANKMENT

CHELSEA BRIDGE

RIVER THAMES

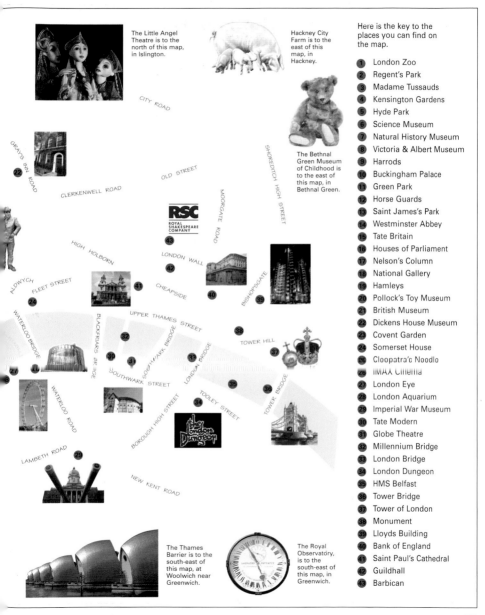

The Little Angel Theatre is to the north of this map, in Islington.

Hackney City Farm is to the east of this map, in Hackney.

The Bethnal Green Museum of Childhood is to the east of this map, in Bethnal Green.

CITY ROAD

GRAYS INN ROAD

SHOREDITCH HIGH STREET

OLD STREET

CLERKENWELL ROAD

MOORGATE ROAD

HIGH HOLBORN

RSC
ROYAL SHAKESPEARE COMPANY

LONDON WALL

ALDWYCH

FLEET STREET

CHEAPSIDE

BISHOPSGATE

WATERLOO BRIDGE

UPPER THAMES STREET

TOWER HILL

BLACKFRIARS BRIDGE

SOUTHWARK BRIDGE

SOUTHWARK STREET

LONDON BRIDGE

TOWER BRIDGE

WATERLOO ROAD

BOROUGH HIGH STREET

TOOLEY STREET

LAMBETH ROAD

NEW KENT ROAD

The Thames Barrier is to the south-east of this map, at Woolwich near Greenwich.

The Royal Observatory, is to the south-east of this map, in Greenwich.

Here is the key to the places you can find on the map.

1. London Zoo
2. Regent's Park
3. Madame Tussauds
4. Kensington Gardens
5. Hyde Park
6. Science Museum
7. Natural History Museum
8. Victoria & Albert Museum
9. Harrods
10. Buckingham Palace
11. Green Park
12. Horse Guards
13. Saint James's Park
14. Westminster Abbey
15. Tate Britain
16. Houses of Parliament
17. Nelson's Column
18. National Gallery
19. Hamleys
20. Pollock's Toy Museum
21. British Museum
22. Dickens House Museum
23. Covent Garden
24. Somerset House
25. Cleopatra's Needle
26. IMAX Cinema
27. London Eye
28. London Aquarium
29. Imperial War Museum
30. Tate Modern
31. Globe Theatre
32. Millennium Bridge
33. London Bridge
34. London Dungeon
35. HMS Belfast
36. Tower Bridge
37. Tower of London
38. Monument
39. Lloyds Building
40. Bank of England
41. Saint Paul's Cathedral
42. Guildhall
43. Barbican

Visitors' guide

The following pages are full of useful information. You can look up the address, telephone number and nearest Underground or rail station for the places mentioned in this book, as well as some more general information. It's always a good idea to check opening times before making a visit, because these are often changed. Remember that some places charge an admission fee, and that many are closed on bank holidays and over Christmas. Official buildings may close for special ceremonies. Most of these places have websites where you can look up opening hours, directions and details of up-coming events. You can find links to these websites at **www.usborne-quicklinks.com**

General information

The Britain and London Visitor Centre
1 Regent Street
London
SW1Y 4XT
Tel. 8846 9000

Most national newspapers have a weekend supplement with detailed information about the films, shows and events going on in London over the following week. Time Out magazine comes out every Tuesday and has the latest listings for London.

Money

British money comes in pounds and pence. There are 100 pence in a pound. Many high street stores now accept payment in euros.

Shop opening hours

Shops are generally open Monday to Saturday, until about 7pm. Many West End shops stay open later on certain nights of the week. Shops in busy areas are often open on Sundays.

Travel information

London Travel
Information
Tel. 7222 1234

Advice for disabled passengers is available from Access Mobility, Windsor House
42-50 Victoria Street
SW1H 0TL
Tel. 7222 1234

To check out train times and see if there are any problems on the railways,
Tel. 08457 484950

London districts

London is divided into districts. Each district is given a postal code by the post

office. You can tell where a place will be from its postal code. For instance, SW means south-west, WC means west-central and E means east. As well as letters, each code has a number. For example, the code for the area around Shaftesbury Avenue is W1. Generally, the higher the number, the farther away the place is from the centre.

Telephones

If you want to find a telephone number, you can ring directory enquiries. You will need to tell them the name and the address, if you know it, of the person or place you want to contact.

Directory enquiries: 118 500

International directory enquiries: 118 505

Operator assistance: 100

Emergency services: 999

To call London from elsewhere in the UK, dial 020 and the number.

To call London from abroad, dial (+44) 20 and the number.

To call abroad from the UK, dial 00, the country code and the number.

Weather information

The Met Office
Tel. 0870 900 0100

London "A to Z"

The London "A to Z" contains detailed maps of every part of the capital. At the back there is a street index, with a map reference, as shown below.

This is the cover of the London "A to Z".

Street name		Map reference	
Garrick St.	WC2	-	3E 60d
	Postal code		Page reference

Places to visit

Pages 4-5
Roman Wall
Saint Alphage's Church Yard, EC2
Tube: Barbican

Queen Boudicca's Statue
Westminster Bridge, W1
Tube: Westminster

Pages 8-9
Shakespeare's Globe
Bankside, SE1
Box office tel. 7401 9919
Front of house tel. 7902 1400
Tube: Southwark

Golden Hinde
Saint Mary Overie Dock
Cathedral Street, SE1
Tel. 0870 011 8700
Tube/Rail: London Bridge

Pages 12-13
One Canada Square Tower
Docklands, E14
Tube: Canary Wharf

30 St Mary Axe
City of London, EC3
Tube/Rail: Liverpool St

London Eye
Southbank, SE1
Tel. 0870 990 8883
Tube/Rail: Waterloo

Tate Modern
See pages 46-47

Millennium Bridge
Tube/Rail: Blackfriars

Pages 14-15
Westminster Abbey
Westminster, SW1
Tel. 7222 5152
Tube: Westminster

Pages 16-17

Houses of Parliament
Westminster, SW1
Tel. 7219 4272
Tube: Westminster

Pages 18-19
Guildhall
Gresham Street, EC2
Tel. 7332 3786
Tube: Bank
Contact the Guildhall for details of **The Knollys Rose Procession** in June, from All-Hallows-by-the-Tower to Mansion House, and **The Presentation of a Boar's Head by Butchers** in December.

Saint Bride's Church
Fleet Street, EC4
Tel. 7427 0133
Tube/Rail: Blackfriars

Monument
Monument Street, EC4
Tel. 7626 2717
Tube: Monument

Lloyds Building
Lime Street, EC3
Tube: Monument

Bank of England Museum
Bartholomew Lane, EC2
Tel. 7601 5545
Tube: Bank

Pages 20-21
Saint Paul's Cathedral
Ludgate Hill, EC4
Tel. 7236 4128
Tube: Saint Paul's

Pages 22-23
HM Tower of London
Tower Hill, EC3
Tel. 0870 756 6060
Tube: Tower Hill

Pages 24-25
Cleopatra's Needle
Victoria Embankment, SW1
Tube: Embankment

London Bridge, SE1
Tube/Rail: London Bridge

Tower Bridge Experience
Tower Bridge, SE1
Tel. 7403 3761
Tube: Tower Hill

Swan-Upping
Starts at Sunbury-on-Thames and finishes at Abingdon Bridge. July.

Doggett's Coat and Badge Race
Starts at London Bridge and finishes at Cadogan Pier, Chelsea. Late July or early August.

Oxford and Cambridge Boat Race
Starts at Putney and finishes at Chiswick. Easter.

Pages 26-27
Covent Garden Market & Jubilee Market
Covent Garden, WC2
Open daily, 9am–5pm, later in the summer
Tube: Covent Garden

Royal Opera House
Bow Street, WC2
Tel. 7304 4000
Tube: Covent Garden

Theatre Royal
Drury Lane, WC2
Tel. 7494 5000
Tube: Covent Garden

Saint Paul's Church
Covent Garden Piazza, WC2
Tel. 7836 5221
Tube: Covent Garden

Seven Dials / Neal's Yard
Monmouth Street, WC2
Tube: Covent Garden

Pages 28-29
Trafalgar Square, WC2
Tube/Rail: Charing Cross

Saint Martin-in-the-Fields Church and the London Brass Rubbing Centre
Trafalgar Square, WC2
Church Tel. 7766 1100
Brass Rubbing Centre
Tel. 7930 9306
Tube/Rail: Charing Cross

National Gallery
See pages 46-47

Pages 30-31
Buckingham Palace, SW1
Tickets for summer opening from Green Park Ticket Office Tel. 7766 7300
Tube: Saint James's Park

Royal Mews
Buckingham Palace Road, SW1
Tel. 7766 7302
Tube/Rail: Victoria

Queen's Gallery
Buckingham Palace Road, SW1
Tel. 7766 7301
Tube/Rail: Victoria

Changing of the Guard
Buckingham Palace
11.30am. Daily in summer, alternate days in winter.
Tube: Victoria/
Saint James's Park

Places to visit

Pages 32-33

Saint James's Park, SW1
Tel. 7930 1793
Tube: Saint James's Park

Green Park, SW1
Tel. 7930 1793
Tube: Green Park

Hyde Park, W1
Tel. 7298 2100
Tube: Hyde Park Corner

**London to Brighton
Car Run**
From Hyde Park Corner.
November.

Kensington Gardens, W1
Tel. 7298 2100
Tube: Lancaster Gate

Kensington Palace
Kensington Gardens, W8
Tel. 0870 751 5170
Tube: High Street Kensington

Pages 34-35

Regent's Park, NW1
Tel. 7486 7905
Tube: Regent's Park

Richmond Park
Richmond, Surrey
Tel. 8948 3209
Tube/Rail: Richmond

Kew Gardens
Kew, Surrey
Tel. 8332 5655
Tube: Kew Gardens

Pages 36-37

Hampton Court
East Molesey, Surrey
Tel. 0870 752 7777
Rail: Hampton Court

DLR = Docklands Light Railway

Royal Observatory
Greenwich, SE10
Tel. 8858 4422
Tube: North Greenwich
DLR: Cutty Sark

**National Maritime
Museum**
Romney Road, SE10
Tel. 8858 4422
Tube: North Greenwich
DLR: Cutty Sark

Thames Barrier
1 Unity Way, SE18
Tel. 8305 4188
Rail: Charlton

Pages 38-39

British Museum
Great Russell Street, WC1
Tel. 7323 8299
Tube:
Tottenham
Court Road

**Pollock's Toy
Museum**
Scala Street,
W1
Tel. 7636 3452
Tube: Goodge Street

**Bethnal Green Museum of
Childhood**
Cambridge Heath Road, E2
Tel. 8983 5200
Tube: Bethnal Green
Rail: Cambridge Heath

Pages 40-41

Natural History Museum
Cromwell Road, SW7
Tel. 7942 5000
Tube: South Kensington

Science Museum
Exhibition Road, SW7
Tel. 7942 5000
Tube: South Kensington

Pages 42-43

Madame Tussauds
Marylebone Road, NW1
Tel. 0870 999 0046
Tube: Baker Street

Emirates Stadium
Drayton Park, N5
Tel. 7704 4000
Tube: Arsenal

**Winston Churchill's
Britain at War Experience**
Tooley Street, SE1
Tel. 7403 3171
Tube/Rail: London Bridge

**Chessington World of
Adventures**
Chessington, Surrey
Tel. 0870 999 0045
Rail: Chessington South

Royal Air Force Museum
Grahame Park Way, NW9
Tel. 8205 2266
Tube: Colindale

BBC Backstage Tours
BBC Television Centre,
Wood Lane, W12
Tel. 0870 603 0304
Tube: White City

Alexandra Palace, N22
Tel. 8365 2121
Tube: Wood Green, then
W3 bus
Rail: Alexandra Palace

Royal Albert Hall
Kensington Gore, SW7
Tel. 7589 8212
Tube: South Kensington

HMS Belfast
Morgans Lane, SE1
Tel. 7940 6300
Tube/Rail: London Bridge

London Dungeon
Tooley Street, SE1
Tel. 7403 7221
Tube/Rail: London Bridge

IMAX Cinema
Charlie Chaplin Walk, SE1
Tel. 0870 787 2525
Tube/Rail: Waterloo

London Butterfly House
Syon Park, Brentford
Tel. 8560 7272
Tube: Gunnersbury, then
bus 237 or 267 to Brent
Lea Gate

**City farms:
Kentish Town City Farm**
Cressfield Close, NW5
Tel. 7916 5420/1
Tube: Kentish Town

Stepping Stones Farm
Stepney Way, E1
Tel. 7790 8204
Tube: Stepney Green

Freightliners Farm
Paradise Park, Sheringham
Road, N7
Tel. 7609 0467
Tube: Holloway Road

Hackney City Farm
Goldsmiths Row,
London, E2
Tel. 7729 6381
Tube: Bethnal Green
Rail: Cambridge Heath

Pages 44-45

Museum of London
London Wall, EC2
Tel. 0870 444 3852
Tube: Barbican

Victoria & Albert Museum
Cromwell Road, SW7
Tel. 7942 2000
Tube. South Kensington

Imperial War Museum
Lambeth Road, SE1
Tel. 7416 5320
Tube: Lambeth North

London Zoo
Regents Park, NW1
Tel. 7722 3333
Tube: Camden Town

London Aquarium
County Hall, Westminster
Bridge Road, SE1
Tel. 7967 8000
Tube: Westminster/Waterloo

Pages 46-47

National Gallery
Trafalgar Square, WC2
Tel. 7747 2885
Tube/Rail: Charing Cross

Tate Britain
Millbank, SW1
Tel. 7887 8888
Tube: Pimlico

Tate Modern
Bankside, SE1
Tel: 7887 8888
Tube: Southwark

Somerset House
The Strand, WC2
Tel: 7845 4600
Tube/Rail: Charing Cross

Barbican
Barbican Centre, EC2
Tel: 7638 4141
Tube: Barbican

National Theatre
South Bank, SE1
Tel: 7452 3000
Tube/Rail: Waterloo

Polka Children's Theatre
The Broadway, Wimbledon,
SW19
Tel. 8543 4888
Tube/Rail: Wimbledon

Unicorn Theatre
Tooley Street, SE1
Tel. 08700 534 534
Tube: Caledonian Road

Little Angel Theatre
Dagmar Passage, N1
Tel. 7226 1787
Tube: Angel

Pages 48-49

Changing of the Guard
Horse Guards Arch, SW1
Monday-Saturday 11am
Sunday 10am
Tube/Rail: Charing Cross

Beating Retreat
Horse Guards Parade, SW1
May or June
Tel. 7839 5323
Tube/Rail: Charing Cross

Trooping the Colour
Horse Guards Parade, SW1
Second Saturday in June
Tel. 7414 2479
Tube/Rail: Charing Cross

Beating the Bounds
Around Tower of London
11am Ascension Day (40th
day after Easter), every 3rd
year (2008, 2011, 2014)
Tel. 3166 6267
Tube: Tower Hill

Pearly Harvest Festival
Saint Martin-in-the-Fields
Trafalgar Square, WC2
First Sunday in October
Tel. 7766 1100
Tube/Rail: Charing Cross

**Trafalgar Square
Christmas Tree**
Trafalgar Square, WC2
Tube/Rail: Charing Cross
December. Carols until
December 25.

**Chinese New Year Lion
Dance**
Gerrard Street, W1
January or February
Tube: Leicester Square

Notting Hill Carnival
Portobello Road area, W10
August Bank Holiday
Tube: Notting Hill/
Ladbroke Grove

Pages 50-51

Dickens House Museum
48 Doughty Street, WC1
Tel. 7405 2127
Tube: Russell Square

**Sherlock Holmes'
Museum**
Baker Street, NW1
Tel. 7935 8866
Tube: Baker Street

Cabinet War Rooms
King Charles Street, SW1
Tel. 7930 6961
Tube: Westminster

Saint Mary-le-Bow Church
Cheapside, EC2
Tel. 7248 5139
Tube: St Paul's

**Statue of Dick
Whittington's
Cat**
Highgate Hill
Tube: Archway

Pages 52-53

Harrods
Knightsbridge, SW1
Tel. 7730 1234
Tube: Knightsbridge

Hamleys
Regent Street, W1
Tel. 0800 2802 444
Tube: Oxford Circus

Fortnum & Mason
Piccadilly, W1
Tel. 7734 8040
Tube: Piccadilly

Liberty's
Regent Street, W1
Tel. 7734 1234
Tube: Oxford Circus

Portobello Market, W10
Every Saturday
Tube: Notting Hill Gate/
Ladbroke Grove

Petticoat Lane Market
Middlesex Street, E1
Sunday mornings
Tube/Rail: Liverpool Street

Leadenhall Market
Gracechurch Street, EC3
Monday to Friday
Tube: Bank/Monument

Berwick Street Market
Berwick Street, W1
Monday to Saturday
Tube: Piccadilly Circus

Brixton Market
Electric Avenue, SW9
Monday to Saturday
Tube: Brixton

Camden Market
Camden, NW1
Thursday to Sunday
Tube: Camden Town

Greenwich Market
College Approach,
Greenwich, SE10
Daily
Tube: North Greenwich
DLR: Cutty Sark

Covent Garden Market
Covent Garden, WC2
Daily
Tube: Covent Garden

Old Spitalfields Market
Commercial Street, E1
Daily, but best on Sunday
Tube/Rail: Liverpool Street

Columbia Road Market
Columbia Road, E2
Sunday mornings
Tube: Shoreditch
Tube/Rail: Old Street

Pages 54-55

**London's Transport
Museum**
Covent Garden, WC2
Tel. 7379 6344
Tube: Covent Garden

Index

Acknowledgements

Every effort has been made to trace the copyright holders of the material in this book. If any rights have been omitted, the publishers offer to rectify this in any future edition, following notification. The publishers are grateful to the following organizations and individuals for their contribution and permission to reproduce material:

PHOTO CREDITS

p2 Ian Britton/Freefoto
p8 The Golden Hinde Museum (tr)
p10 National Gallery, Prague/AKG London (t)
p11 Ian Britton/Freefoto (mr)
p12 London City Airport Ltd. (bl); ©Mary Quant Ltd. (ml); ©Martin Jones/Corbis (br)
p14 Collections/Malcolm Crowthers, courtesy of Westminster Abbey (tl)
p15 Collections/Malcolm Crowthers (tr)
p19 Corporation of London
p20 Ian Britton/Freefoto (l); Rex Features (r)
p21 Philip Way (tr)
p22 Collections/James Bartholomew (tl)
p23 Royal Holloway and Bedford New College, Surrey/Bridgeman Art Library (bl)
p24-25 David Paterson/Getty One Stone (t)
p27 ©Robbie Jack/Corbis (tl); ©Seven Dials (mr); Rex Features (br)
p29 London Brass Rubbing Centre (br)
p32 ©London Aerial Photo Library/Corbis (l); ©Michael John Kielty/Corbis (mr)
p34 Powerstock Zefa (l); ©Michael Nicholson/Corbis (tr)
p35 ©Angelo Hornak/Corbis (b); ©Jeremy Horner/Corbis (mr)
p36 Pictures Colour Library (bl); ©Rupert Horrox/Corbis (br)
p37 ©Adam Woolfitt/Corbis (mr)
p38 ©British Museum
p39 ©Trustees of the Victoria & Albert Museum (t)
p40 The Natural History Museum, London
p41 The Science Museum

p42 Photos courtesy of Madame Tussauds London (l); ©www.arsenalpics.com (ml); Britain at War Experience (tm); BBC Backstage Tours (bm)
p43 London Dungeon (l); ©RAF Museum (tr); Chessington World of Adventures (br)
p44 Victoria and Albert Museum (l); Museum of London (r)
p45 The London Aquarium (t); ©Zoological Society of London (b)
p46 Peter Durant/arcblue.com (bl); Courtauld Gallery, London (m); National Gallery, London (tr)
p47 Nick Liseiko/The Hackney Empire (ml); Tony Wallis/Little Angel Theatre (bl); photograph by Stephen Cummiskey (tr); The Royal Shakespeare Company (mr); Tristram Kenton/Apollo Victoria Theatre (br)
p48 Sgt. Ian Liptrot, Media Ops London District (l, tr); Collections/Brian Shuel (mr); Pat and Carole Jolly (br)
p49 Collections/Brian Shuel (tl); Notting Hill Carnival Trust Press Office (bl); ©Adam Carroll/Eye Ubiquitus/Corbis (tr, br); London Tourist Board (mr)
p50 Pat and Carole Jolly (br)
p51 ©Robert Estall/Corbis (m); Cabinet War Rooms (b)
p52 Harrods Ltd. (t); London Tourist Board (bl); Hamleys of London (br)
p53 ©Rupert Horrox/Corbis (tr); ©Jan Butchofsky/Corbis (mr); Collections/Dominic Cole (bl)
p55 Photo courtesy of Eurostar (tl); BAA Picture Library of BAA plc (mr); London Transport Museum (b)
p56-57 (where not previously credited) Hamleys of London; Madame Tussauds London; London Dungeon; Tony Wallis; ©Trustees of the Victoria & Albert Museum; The Royal Shakespeare Company
p58 Geographers' A-Z Map Company (br)

Additional contributors

Additional photography by:	Brian Voakes
Additional designs by:	Lucy Owen
Digital manipulation:	John Russell, Brian Voakes
Picture research by:	Ruth King
Additional illustrations by:	Linda Penny, Joe McEwan, Terence Dalley, Guy Smith, Kim Blundell, Ross Watton
Editorial assistance:	Fiona Patchett, Hazel Maskell